# JUST
# JESUS
# THEM

*The Way to reignite your spiritual fire within.*

## JOHN STAHL

Copyright © 2016 by John Stahl

*Just JESUS Them*
*The Way to reignite your spiritual fire within.*
by John Stahl

Email: Contact us at JustJESUSThem@gmail.com
Follow us on Twitter: @JustJESUSThem
Like us on Facebook: A Pocket Full of Faith

Printed in the United States of America.
Edited by Xulon Press.

ISBN 9781498462051

All rights reserved solely by the author. The author guarantees all contents are original and do not infringe upon the legal rights of any other person or work. No part of this book may be reproduced in any form without the permission of the author. The views expressed in this book are not necessarily those of the publisher.

Unless otherwise indicated, Scripture quotations taken from the Living Bible (TLB). Copyright © 1971 by Tyndale House Foundation. Used by permission of Tyndale House Publishers Inc., Carol Stream, Illinois 60188. All rights reserved.

Scripture quotations taken from the Holy Bible, New Living Translation (NLT). Copyright ©1996, 2004, 2007 by Tyndale House Foundation. Used by permission of Tyndale House Publishers, Inc.

Scripture quotations taken from the New King James Version (NKJV). Copyright © 1982 by Thomas Nelson, Inc. Used by permission. All rights reserved.

Scripture quotations taken from the Holy Bible, New International Version (NIV). Copyright © 1973, 1978, 1984, 2011 by Biblica, Inc.™. Used by permission. All rights reserved.

Scripture quotations taken from the English Standard Version (ESV). Copyright © 2001 by Crossway, a publishing ministry of Good News Publishers. Used by permission. All rights reserved.

Scripture quotations taken from the Good News Translation (GNT). Copyright ©1995 by Baker Publishing Group.

Scripture quotations taken from The Voice Bible Copyright © 2012 Thomas Nelson, Inc. The Voice™ translation © 2012 Ecclesia Bible Society All rights reserved.

Scripture quotations taken from New Life Version (NLV). Copyright © 1969 by Christian Literature International.

www.xulonpress.com

From: Donna Anderson
4/3/16

# SPECIAL THANKS:

To Deanna, Lisa, and Ben. They JESUS others and they were my first editors. Thanks for sticking with me! I JESUS you!

To Hernan. Your words called me to action. I JESUS you, my friend!

To Tom, who kept me accountable: "I think I'd like to get to know that guy a little better." That is how JESUSing others starts.

To my wife, Deanna, who was also one of my editors, my children Chandler, Jacob, Nathan, and Becca, for allowing me to clutter your world for awhile as I finished this book. I believe you all show me how important it is to JESUS others more than you know!

To Chris Kaczmar, Dallas, Tim, Chris Zabel, Glenn, Tandy, Keith, P-Scotty, Pastor Jeff, Jody, Rich and Karrie, my High Point Christian Church family, and the many others that JESUSed me along the way. My fear is I will miss someone personally. If I did, I apologize. Don't let that stop you from JESUSing others. I will just have to JESUS you even more!

When you turn the page, be ready to act. This is not a devotional. It is a 'DO'-votional.

And remember: I JESUS YOU! Now it is your turn.

Just JESUS Them.

# Table of Contents

| | | |
|---|---|---|
| Day 1 | *Spelling love..* | 14 |
| Day 2 | *Motivating others.* | 16 |
| Day 3 | *Loving love..* | 18 |
| Day 4 | *Living in the present..* | 20 |
| Day 5 | *Playing a game..* | 22 |
| Day 6 | *Sending a text message..* | 24 |
| Day 7 | *JOURNALING* | 26 |
| Day 8 | *Smiling at someone.* | 28 |
| Day 9 | *Spending time with family..* | 30 |
| Day 10 | *Making eye contact.* | 32 |
| Day 11 | *Mending a relationship..* | 34 |
| Day 12 | *Scratching a back.* | 36 |
| Day 13 | *Following directions..* | 38 |
| Day 14 | *JOURNALING* | 40 |
| Day 15 | *Watching a movie.* | 42 |
| Day 16 | *Breaking bread together.* | 44 |
| Day 17 | *Dealing with death..* | 46 |
| Day 18 | *Reading a love letter.* | 48 |
| Day 19 | *Picking up the phone..* | 50 |
| Day 20 | *Giving money to a homeless person..* | 52 |
| Day 21 | *JOURNALING* | 54 |
| Day 22 | *Reaching someone who has lost his or her 'Way.'* | 56 |
| Day 23 | *Sending a card or note.* | 58 |
| Day 24 | *Playing through pain..* | 60 |
| Day 25 | *Making time to pray..* | 62 |
| Day 26 | *Visiting a friend.* | 64 |
| Day 27 | *Bringing fairness to life..* | 66 |
| Day 28 | *JOURNALING* | 68 |
| Day 29 | *Coaching a team.* | 70 |
| Day 30 | *Saying nothing at all.* | 72 |
| Day 31 | *Making the most of THIS day.* | 74 |
| Day 32 | *Making an introduction.* | 76 |
| Day 33 | *Laughing to laugh..* | 78 |
| Day 34 | *Telling a story.* | 80 |
| Day 35 | *JOURNALING* | 82 |
| Day 36 | *Being bold.* | 84 |
| Day 37 | *Breaking fear.* | 86 |
| Day 37 | *Taking a step..* | 88 |
| Day 39 | *Producing fruit.* | 90 |

| | | |
|---|---|---|
| **Day 40** | Putting your faith into action. | 92 |
| **Day 41** | Celebrating with others. | 94 |
| **Day 42** | JOURNALING | 96 |
| **Day 43** | Taking back the dinner table. | 98 |
| **Day 44** | Doing yard work. | 100 |
| **Day 45** | RANDOM ACT OF KINDNESS (Part 1) | 102 |
| **Day 46** | RANDOM ACT OF KINDNESS (Part 2) | 104 |
| **Day 47** | RANDOM ACT OF KINDNESS (Part 3) | 106 |
| **Day 48** | Appreciating others. | 108 |
| **Day 49** | JOURNALING | 110 |
| **Day 50** | Finishing Third. | 112 |
| **Day 51** | Giving a hug. | 114 |
| **Day 52** | Raising your hands. | 116 |
| **Day 53** | Walking in prayer. | 118 |
| **Day 54** | Achieving Balance. | 120 |
| **Day 55** | Holding a hand. | 122 |
| **Day 56** | JOURNALING | 124 |
| **Day 57** | Asking a question. | 126 |
| **Day 58** | Attending calling hours or a funeral. | 128 |
| **Day 59** | Being who God made you to be. | 130 |
| **Day 60** | Listening in the living room. | 132 |
| **Day 61** | Doing something simple. | 134 |
| **Day 62** | Stop pretending. | 136 |
| **Day 63** | JOURNALING | 138 |
| **Day 64** | Fearing no more. | 140 |
| **Day 65** | Experiencing JOY. | 142 |
| **Day 66** | Avoiding JOYsuckers. | 144 |
| **Day 67** | Donating your self. | 146 |
| **Day 68** | Finding Beauty. | 148 |
| **Day 69** | Throwing a ball. | 150 |
| **Day 70** | JOURNALING | 152 |
| **Day 71** | Taking the first step. | 154 |
| **Day 72** | Being prepared. | 156 |
| **Day 73** | Loving your neighbor. | 158 |
| **Day 74** | Explaining Salvation (Part 1) | 160 |
| **Day 75** | Explaining Salvation (Part 2) | 162 |
| **Day 76** | Sharing heaven. | 164 |
| **Day 77** | JOURNALING | 166 |
| **Day 78** | Adopting a child. | 168 |
| **Day 79** | Timing is everything. | 170 |
| **Day 80** | Living with resolve. | 172 |
| **Day 81** | Looking with our heart. | 174 |

| | | |
|---|---|---|
| Day 82 | Living your dash. | 176 |
| Day 83 | Killing sacred cows. | 178 |
| Day 84 | JOURNALING | 180 |
| Day 85 | Making it last. | 182 |
| Day 86 | (Part 1) Making a visit. | 184 |
| Day 87 | (Part 2) Battling life. | 186 |
| Day 88 | (Part 3) Sharing good news. | 188 |
| Day 89 | (Part 4) Knocking on a door. | 190 |
| Day 90 | Showing tough love. | 192 |
| Day 91 | JOURNALING | 194 |
| Day 92 | Dealing with divorce. | 196 |
| Day 93 | Making a first impression. | 198 |
| Day 94 | Asking questions. | 200 |
| Day 95 | Filling a God-Shaped Hole. | 202 |
| Day 96 | Weathering the storm. | 204 |
| Day 97 | Seeing God. | 206 |
| Day 98 | JOURNALING | 208 |
| Day 99 | Wanting less. | 210 |
| Day 100 | Being a light. | 212 |
| Day 101 | (Part 1) Breaking the ice. | 214 |
| Day 102 | (Part 2) Breaking the ice. | 216 |
| Day 103 | Avoiding distractions. | 218 |
| Day 104 | Having a "Plan B". | 220 |
| Day 105 | JOURNALING | 222 |
| Day 106 | (Part 1) Sharing Jesus not the church. | 224 |
| Day 107 | (Part 2) Sharing Jesus not the church. | 226 |
| Day 108 | Living for a cause. | 228 |
| Day 109 | Gaining Trust. | 230 |
| Day 110 | Taking accountability. | 232 |
| Day 111 | Knowing whom we serve. | 234 |
| Day 112 | JOURNALING | 236 |
| Day 113 | Spending your resources. | 238 |
| Day 114 | Making a choice. | 240 |
| Day 115 | Praying with purpose. | 242 |
| Day 116 | Including everyone. | 244 |
| Day 117 | Overcoming addictions. | 246 |
| Day 118 | Battling depression. | 248 |
| Day 119 | JOURNALING | 250 |
| Day 120 | Investing in people. | 252 |
| Day 121 | Forgetting God. | 254 |
| Day 122 | Playing to win. | 256 |

# The daily DO-votional breakdown:

**YOUR Day** *(EVERY Day is different. This is your day from God. What will you do with it?)*
*Loving as JESUS loved moment. (The THEME behind the day—our role is to CHALLENGE you.)* _____

Your JESUSing Moment *(Where you make this personal, this is the 'what' and 'where'—this is where you allow God to CHANGE you.)*

_____ Date *(Write it down so you do not forget the 'when.')*

*James 1:22(The Message) Don't fool yourself into thinking that you are a listener when you are anything but, letting the Word go in one ear and out the other. ACT on what you hear! (The message behind the message you live for the day. This is the 'why.')*

"Just Do It." ™

This is possibly the most famous, distinct, and simple slogan in history. Famous because it comes from the Nike brand, which is a worldwide success story. Distinct because it speaks to each of us, yet calls us to make a decision to act. Simple because it is three words that you and I can remember and relate.

So what is "it" to you? What is "it" that you need to do? Deep in your heart, something stirs when you read those words. You know "it" is there and "it" wants to come out and be alive. For most of us, "it" lies dormant. For most of us "it" dares us to do more. "It" dares us to be more. "It" dares us to live not as we do now, but as God wants us to live.

This book is not just a devotional. It is a DOvotional. It is a call to action and to bring hope to a seemingly hopeless world, one act of love, one JESUSing moment at a time. Only *you* know that hope that lives within you. Only *you* can live that hope. Only *you* can give that hope away to those that you love.

How do we do this? The first step is to take a *specific* action. We take action by changing **JESUS** from a **NOUN** to a **VERB**. When you Jesus others, you love others as Jesus loved others. Your vocabulary, your walk, and your talk will change every time you stop long enough to SHOW someone these words: *"I Jesus you."*

One final challenge: do not worry about changing the world. Start with your world. Start with those around you in your work, school, community, teams, and neighborhoods. When you change your world, and others change their worlds, it gets contagious. Who knows, maybe, in the end, God changes so many people's worlds that the whole world cannot help but change. It starts with each of us, however, individually.

But, don't just listen and read. Act on it.

Just Jesus Them.

*JESUSing moment>>> Each and every day there will be a note at the bottom that is meant for you and God to walk together. It is meant to give you ideas and challenge you to meet someone right where they are. It may not be a well, or temple, or marketplace, but will be where your life takes you. Where you meet Jesus that day and take it to someone you may not even know, or may have known for years. It is the opportunity to love that person. When those two worlds collide, that is your JESUSing moment. Also, at the bottom of the page is a postage-stamp size QR code. You can scan these daily from your smart phone to watch a brief, one minute video that is about the scripture from the day. (This will become your "how' based on your 'who,' which will change daily, or the who could remain constant. You choose. Every day. When you turn the page, be ready to act. Time to start your DO-votional.)*

*Just JESUS Them*

# Day 1  4/3/16
*Spelling love.*

---

Your JESUSing Moment                                           Date

**Psalm 90:12 (TLB) *Teach us to number our days and recognize how few they are; help us to spend them as we should.***

If you have ever wondered how kids spell the word love it is not what you would think. Conventional wisdom would say to us it is L–O–V–E. A trip to the dictionary would confirm the spelling. Modernists would spell it like this: L-U-V. We would all be wrong.

So, what is the correct spelling? Here it is: T-I-M-E.

Time. More than anything, children want to spend time with those they care the most about in their lives. At a younger age, that is usually their siblings and parents. As they grow older, this changes to friends. Sadly, this is the time that parents lose touch with their children. Even sadder is that parents justify this loss of time with their kids. At some point one or a few events have taken place. The parents are no longer cool. The kids need their space. The kids are just 'going through a phase' or are going through puberty. I could continue to list excuse after excuse. In the end that is all they are: excuses.

I remember reading a story once about a dad who lost touch with his son. His wife had shared with him how little time the two spent together. The dad was so busy making a living and providing for his family he lost track of the most important need for his son: T-I-M-E. At first the dad was offended by the comment his wife had made. He was more than a little put off and did not talk to his wife the rest of the day. As he thought through the evening and the next day about their conversation, he came to a surprising realization. She was right.

His son's birthday was only a few weeks away. Rather than get him the latest game, brand-name shoes, tickets to a concert or show that he could attend with his friends, he gave his son the best gift he could. He gave him the gift of T-I-M-E.

His son opened the gift that his dad had given him. Inside the box was a watch with a note. It said: *"For the next year I'm giving you the gift of TIME. Every day for 30 minutes you and I will spend TIME together. Just the two of us."*

The next year found father and son spending T-I-M-E together every day. 30 minutes turned into an hour, which turned into two hours and the relationship between the father and his teenage son grew and grew. A year went by and the son's next birthday was once again approaching. The teenagers' mom asked her son what he would like for his next birthday.

His response? "I already have everything I could ever ask for." With that, he went out to greet his dad who was coming home from work so they could have their TIME together.

***JESUSing moment>>> T-I-M-E. It is how we spell love. It doesn't have to be our children that we spend it with, either. Who is in your life that you can go and JESUS TODAY by giving them this awesome gift?***

www.PocketFullOfFaith.com

*Just JESUS Them*

# Day 2 4/4/16
*Motivating others.*

---

Your JESUSing Moment                                    Date

**Mark 6:7a (NLT) And he called his twelve disciples together and began sending them out two by two.**

You cannot motivate those who do not want to be motivated. It was the first lesson I was ever taught in ministry. The idea behind it was very simple. There are a lot of people who say that they want to do things. At the end of the day there are very few who actually do them. I would love tell you that I learned this lesson easily. Looking back after years of being a business owner, coach, mentor, friend, and church leader, I can tell you this statement is 100 percent accurate.

So the question is, how do we motivate others to the point that they take action? We can say all of the right words. We can be as encouraging as possible. We can give all the best examples and share real life experiences. We can share inspiring quotes, lives of people who made a difference, and Bible verses. All of these things others can relate to and desire to have a part of their lives. At the end of the day they choose whether or not to actually live by these principles in their lives. It is up to them whether or not they choose to be motivated, whether as a spouse, sibling, friend, coworker, student, or a leader.

Jesus gives a great example of how to motivate others in the Bible. Re-read the verse for today. When Jesus sent his disciples out he did not send them alone. He sent the disciples out with a partner "two by two." Too often in this life we try to do things on our own. When we have someone join us, those times are often enjoyable. We point back to those moments and how relationships grew through them. Yet, for some strange reason, the *next* time we attempt to start something, we choose to start it all alone.

Doing it alone masks itself in many ways. For some, they want to quit smoking or drinking. Some would love to lose weight. Others desire to start exercising. Still others hope to get closer to God. These are just a few of the examples people resolve to do or change in their lives. Many times they fail, and find themselves starting over again at some point. Why?

Is it a lack of motivation? Is it a lack of discipline? Is it a lack of self-control? The answer is it could be one or all of these. Everyone is different. Until we have that special someone we can turn to in our lives that has the same passion we have, we will never have the motivation to follow through and change. Sadly, doing it alone means we will continue to have the same results.

If you have a desire to finally change, here is the lesson to learn today: *You cannot motivate those that do not want to be motivated.* If you have read this far that means you are motivated to change. It is now time to get someone to walk alongside of you. It is time to go, and grow, "two by two."

**JESUSing moment>>> Pick something that you have struggled with and quit too many times to count. Pray about the person that God can bring you to help keep your motivation. Now reach out to that person and see if they have the motivation to walk alongside you and head out and do as JESUS did when he sent his disciples two by two.**

www.PocketFullOfFaith.com

*Just JESUS Them*

# Day 3
*Loving love.*

---

Your JESUSing Moment                                              Date

**1 John 4:8 (NIV) Whoever does not love does not know God, because God is love.**

It was March 17, 1995 and Megan Kasmar was coming into this world. Any baby will bring a smile and, for her parents, so much more. This was their little girl. For those of you who have daughters—you know what I mean. For those of you who are daughters, know that you are someone's little girl.

Nick and Patrick were all boy. There was something special about them. I can never remember a time when they were not smiling, goofing around, playing hard, joking and, well, just being boys. I was one of their baseball coaches. They were fun to be around and fun to coach. At the same time, they had a little sister who had gone through a ton of sickness, vomiting, and health struggles. That little sister was Megan.

This is also when I first met their mom, Nadine. She loved her boys, and her little girl, but how she was able to do it on her own, well, no one knows. Yet there she was, always supportive, and always finding a way to smile. She loved who ever was in her path, and always found time for people. She especially loved children and always looked out for them. Not just her kids. EVERY kid. She lived what we all wish we understood: God IS love.

It was March 17, 2011. Megan was turning 16. This is a day that everyone looks forward to. Sweet sixteen's are special. But for this little girl, it was anything but, because this was her last day with us. Megan lost a battle that you would not want any child to go through, as her lungs were no longer able to breathe. We all wished we had the words to say to her mom, to her dad, and to her brothers. The words never came. In the end, all anyone could do was listen and love.

*Just JESUS Them*

Have you ever had that person that you will think of when you hear the word love? For many, that person is Megan. During her sicknesses, she never seemed angry. She never got down. She always looked for the best in others, regardless of who they were, where they were from, male or female, or the color of their skin.

Why? Because Megan loved Jesus. She *LOVED* Him. And this is what Jesus did for Megan: He loved her back. In the end, she even shared this quote with those she came in contact, those she loved (who were many):

"I love, love." ~Megan Nicole Kasmar

Do you love, love? Do you believe God is love? Then go *do* as Jesus did, and love someone today. You may be the only Jesus they see. When you do, you, like Megan, will love, love, too.

***JESUSing moment>>> This is a simple process: LOVE love! Love to LOVE! JESUS = love. Love others. JESUS others.***

*www.PocketFullOfFaith.com*

*Just JESUS Them*

# Day 4
*Living in the present.*

---

*Your JESUSing Moment*                       *Date*

**Isaiah 43:18–19 (NIV) "Forget the former things; do not dwell on the past. See, I am doing a new thing! Now it springs up; do you not perceive it? I am making a way in the wilderness and streams in the wasteland.**

"I cannot get over my past."

I hear this phrase from people often. There is something inside that they cannot seem to get by and they relive it over and over. It may be a relationship, such as a divorce. It could be poor financial decisions that have led to current financial ruin. It could be marrying the wrong person (many times due to their faith not being equal). Another issue might be complacency, such as sitting back and saying or doing nothing when most needed. There is always the ever-present throwing a life away because of addictions such as alcohol, smoking, or drugs. Regardless of the struggle, this is where they live. Daily. Yet, as each day goes by the struggle does not get further away. Instead it festers, and pops up over and over in our minds and then travels to our hearts. The hurt sets in and the vicious claws of our past flare up and dig themselves in and paralyze us.

In order to combat this, you need to understand that there is actually a vicious cycle that is taking place. Many times that cycle starts with anger. You are angry over being hurt or making poor decisions in your past. The anger then leads to hurt. The hurt settles in our heart and our mind and we struggle with it over and over. It is at this point we hit a fork in the road. This is where we make a choice.

One road leads inward and downward. It is our road and we travel it alone. The other road leads outward and upward. This road can be traveled with someone else or many others by your side. The lonely road keeps you in the past. The open road brings you to the present and, eventually, the future.

The sad thing is this the cycle never stops. Something reminds us of that past struggle, hurt, or deficiency. The anger sets in, followed by the hurt, and we find ourselves at that fork in the road. Remember, it is you and I that have to make the choice at this fork in the road *every* time. What we choose is as simple as this: do you want to live angry and hurt every day? Choosing this path leads to bitterness. Sadly, we take this path alone.

Or, do you want to heal and see the new life that God has in store for you? God has shown every believer a new life. Choosing God at the fork in the road leads to healing. You live life with others, including a passionate, personal savior when you choose God in your present.

What will you choose today?

*JESUSing moment>>> If this describes you, it is time to get up and care for someone. The only way to get out of this vicious cycle is to pour your self into another person. It takes you from paralyzed in your past to living in your present.*

www.PocketFullOfFaith.com

# Day 5
*Playing a game.*

---

Your JESUSing Moment                                    Date

**Hebrews 12:1(b) (NLT) And let us run with endurance the race God has set before us.**

Recently our family was to take a 'vacation' to Tennessee for a baseball tournament. Whenever you stay in the area we went to, you have to rent a cabin. For us, renting a cabin in the mountains there means one thing: game time. When we look at the rental sites, one of the first things we check out and require is a billiards/pool table. This strikes me as comical, since we do not even own a pool table at the house in which we live the other 358 days of the year.

Sadly, this year had some twists and turns. It is what we all call life. Instead of a week's vacation with our family of six, it ended up being just me and my youngest son Nate; who was 13 years old at the time. We had to go for two very important reasons: first, he was a player, and second, I was a coach.

What was the first thing my son did as soon as we got in the cabin? He made a dash for the pool table. For four days we played pool (scientifically known as billiards). We tried trick shots and played eight ball and worked on bank shots and had fun. On this trip I got to teach him my favorite game on the table: nine-ball.

For those of you that have never played, you only use balls one through nine. You set the balls up in the rack in order, except the nine-ball is in the center (in the same spot the eight ball would be in regular billiards). If you break and the nine-ball goes in, you win. If not, you have to start in order with the lowest ball on the table (should any ball go in on the break) and go in order (and you HAVE to hit the lowest ball first each and every time it is your turn) until you get to the nine-ball. The nine-ball is the only ball you have to call the pocket for, as well. Slop counts (which is great for our games). Here is the kicker: at ANY time, if the nine-ball goes in while you are hitting any other ball, you win (as long as you do not scratch on the same shot—then you lose).

The game is fast paced and fun. You can be completely dominating and knock in the first eight balls and then lose the game because you missed the nine ball. Or, you can be playing horribly and then accidentally hit a ball and the nine-ball falls in a pocket. The first way is frustrating, the second *way* better.

Regardless, the memories and joy built on this trip were great for baseball. But, the time spent together in the cabin working on our nine-ball skills (or lack of them), were what Jesus would smile upon the most.

***JESUSing moment>>> Go and play a game you enjoy with someone! Competition gets the juices flowing. Love someone by competing with him/her BUT make sure to love first—just as Jesus did!***

www.PocketFullOfFaith.com

## Day 6

*Sending a text message.*

✓ _____  _____

Your JESUSing Moment                           Date

**John 8:6b-7 (NIV) But Jesus bent down and started to write on the ground with his finger. When they kept on questioning him, he straightened up and said to them, "Let any one of you who is without sin be the first to throw a stone at her." Again he stooped down and wrote on the ground.**

Whenever I read these verses, I cannot help but think we are witnessing Jesus writing the first text message. After Jesus responds to the crowd, we then get to see Jesus write message number two.

I recently took a look at my cell phone bill. I was checking the number of text messages I had sent in a month while comparing those to that of my teenagers. My wife was over 1,000. I was over 2,000. One of my sons was over 3,000. Between the three of us we were sending roughly 200 text messages a day.

This got me thinking. How many of those text messages are used for good? How often do I send a text message that has meaning for the person on the other end?

I have a friend, Jim, who sends me a Bible verse every day. In it, Jim challenges me to live as the verse teaches. He shares with me how he is going to do the same challenge he sent to me. I find these inspiring, uplifting, and thought provoking.

Jim told me he does not send many text messages. I know when I get a text message from him it was written with care and intent. It was not full of abbreviations or text message jargon. It was from the heart and it was meant to reach me on another level. Something as simple and free as sending a text message telling someone they were on your heart can make someone feel so loved.

It is simple for you.

It is a blessing to them.

*JESUSing moment>>> None of us know what Jesus wrote in the sand that day. All we know for sure is that it had eternal value. It was, after all, Jesus writing. Challenge yourself to send text messages that have meaning. This could be to a friend or neighbor who has lost a loved one. This could be to a coworker who is traveling right now. It could be to a spouse, your child, or for someone in the family who just needs to know that you were thinking of them and that you love them. It is one of the ways we can love others just as Jesus loved us.*

www.PocketFullOfFaith.com

## Day 7

*Take this day to journal. Look back on the past week and share some of the JESUSing moments with yourself. Why? To look back at these later. To reflect. To remember. One day, you may need these moments. It may be a dry time in your spiritual walk; you may feel lonely, or discouraged. By writing your moments when you loved/JESUSed others, you will have those special memories when all that mattered were the God moments your faith showed.*

*Just JESUS Them*

*www.PocketFullOfFaith.com*

*Just JESUS Them*

## Day 8
*Smiling at someone.*

| Your JESUSing Moment | Date |
|---|---|

***Job 29:21-25 (The Message)** "Men and women listened when I spoke, hung expectantly on my every word. After I spoke, they'd be quiet, taking it all in. They welcomed my counsel like spring rain, drinking it all in. When I smiled at them, they could hardly believe it; their faces lit up, their troubles took wing! I was their leader, establishing the mood and setting the pace by which they lived. Where I led, they followed."*

There are certain moments that you run through over and over in your mind. Most times, they do not creep back into your mind until a similar event takes place to take you *back* to that original moment. Let me see if I can explain this better with a story.

A few years ago, I was driving down a routinely busy road when I saw a turtle. It was too busy to stop hard, so I proceeded to the next driveway to turn around and go back to the turtle. After I got out of my car, I noticed just how busy the road was. For some reason it seemed as though the traffic had picked up and that everyone in town must have heard that this turtle was crossing the road.

I was not able to cross the road due to the heavy traffic, and watched as car after car passed over this slow moving turtle. Finally, one car came so close that the turtle dove back into its shell. With just a few cars to go, I saw a break to get across the road. I made it across, and, as I did, I saw the final two cars cross over the turtle. I watched in horror as the last car ran over and crushed the little turtle. This was neither my pet nor a family member, but I was crushed, too. I could not believe that someone would be so insensitive and not pay attention to the road after so many others in front of them had just done so.

Recently, I went back to that moment when I saw a lady crossing a busy intersection. The look on her face said she was bound and determined to make it across the road as she was carrying

*Just JESUS Them*

something. I saw her car parked across the road on the shoulder. When I looked back at her I saw that what she was clutching was, in fact, a turtle.

I waited long enough for her to come out of the waist-high grass by the lake to give her a message. "Thank you for taking the time to save that turtle. You just made my day," I called out to her. She grinned from ear-to-ear and simply nodded her head to me. It was enough for her to make a difference saving the turtle, but her smile and nodding her head to me showed how much she cared. In that moment, this woman took the time to JESUS me (and saved the turtle in the process–which is pretty much a win-win in my book).

**JESUSing moment>>> *Many times we feel our actions have to be huge tokens of work or service to make a difference. Yet, there is something so complete in simply smiling at someone. Take the time today to smile and/or nod your head to people as you pass by them. Notice them for who they are and WHOSE they are. You will Jesus them in those very brief moments. You may even find yourself being JESUSed back!***

www.PocketFullOfFaith.com

## Day 9

*Spending time with family.*

---

Your JESUSing Moment                                                Date

**1 John 5:2 (GNT) This is how we know that we love God's children: it is by loving God and obeying his commands.**

(I realize that some people that are reading this may not have kids. Likewise, your kids may be grown and you think this day is not for you. But, we all have nieces/nephews/grandkids or even our spouse that we can reach out to, so you do not get a free pass on this day!)

Recently we had a perfect storm happen for our family. All four of our kids had a baseball/softball game in the same community at roughly the same time on the same day. I was planning out the evening to run from field to field (all within a mile of each other) and at-bat by at-bat.

That is when the next storm hit. As is often seen and felt in Ohio in May, the thunder rolled in and the heavens opened up and dropped rain onto the fields. Being a coach myself, I went online to check the radar. This storm was not something that was going to go away anytime soon.

At this point I made an immediate decision. I dropped the rest of my work for the couple of hours left in the day and started to prepare dinner. As each child rolled in off the bus I made sure they jumped on and completed their daily homework. The oldest two children had their impromptu baseball practice cut short, as the head baseball coach was too busy to be at practice.

They, too, finished homework and set the table. Dinner was on the table when their mom got home from work. We enjoyed our meal together, and talked about the day's events. Afterward, two of the kids cleared the table while one unloaded the dishwasher and another loaded it. My wife washed the dishes and I wiped down the table.

*Just JESUS Them*

After cleaning up, the entire family loaded into the minivan (one of the greater inventions known to any family with more than one child) and headed out to see a movie together. The movie we chose was 'God's NOT dead.' We purposefully went to a movie that was a little further away from the house so we could talk about it on the way home, allowing us the time to talk about and answer questions the movie brought to our minds and hearts.

Best.
Storm.
Day.
Ever.

***JESUSing moment>>> Too often we take the time to love others, and we think that the "others" are in our community, at our workplace, or in our schools. We need to remember to love those that we live with, as well! MAKE time today with your family or a family that you are close to who could use a little JESUSing.***

www.PocketFullOfFaith.com

*Just JESUS Them*

## Day 10
*Making eye contact.*

✓ _____ _____
Your JESUSing Moment                                                     Date

**Ephesians 2:8 (ESV) For by grace you have been saved through faith. And this is not your own doing; it is the gift of God**

One task that people hate that I enjoy is grocery shopping. The part I do not like, however is taking too much time to grocery shop. I think most people are in the same boat as it is rare that anyone makes eye contact. People leave their carts in the middle of the aisle as if they are the only ones in the store. And, when they finally notice, they refuse to look at you to move or acknowledge they are in the way. They look down at the ground or back to the shelves and take their time in freeing up the aisle.

Recently, I was on a trip through a local 'mom and pop' grocery store. I was in the home stretch, or what most people would call the final aisle. I was within the allotted time I had set aside to shop, and the only thing left was milk and bread and I was home free to the cash register. Standing in front of the bread was a woman I knew from the community. Michelle purposefully covered her eyes to not look at me. She was joking, and we both laughed, and I knew she was on a timeframe as well. Between our two families, we have nine kids, and it was approaching that time of day where dinners had to be cooked!

After making light of Michelle not wanting to look at me, a conversation took place that led to something even deeper: the fragileness of life. What started as a joke led to a 20 to 30-minute discussion of raising kids, loving our spouses, and struggles we all live with each and every day. It also showed how easy it is to feel guilt in areas of our lives we do not even recognize. Thankfully, this conversation led to a discussion of grace and how God wants us to live our lives through that unending grace.

To think this all started by looking for the bread. Our conversation continued when BOTH parties made eye contact. Guilt was replaced with grace, and God showed up in a way that can only point to Him.

As I walked away from our conversation, I put two loaves of bread in my cart. The next lady that passed me in the aisle was the mother of a child I coached for many years. She was in the home-stretch, as well, but chose to pretend I was not even there. As she hustled for the cash register, I stopped to thank God for the 20–30 minutes I had with my other friend to talk about life.

Had we not MADE eye contact, that discussion would have never taken place, and I would have missed a JESUSing moment that I did not see coming.

*JESUSing moment>>> You would be amazed at how few people want to make eye contact. Today, look to make eye contact with every person you encounter. Be prepared for very few to look back at you. For the ones that do—just smile and even say 'Hello.' WHEN you come across someone that wants to talk, take the time to do so. It can be about something specific, or nothing at all.*

www.PocketFullOfFaith.com

*Just JESUS Them*

# Day 11
*Mending a relationship.*

---

Your JESUSing Moment                                                   Date

**John 21:17 (NIV) He said to him the third time, "Simon, son of John, do you love me?" Peter was grieved because he said to him the third time, "Do you love me?" and he said to him, "Lord, you know everything; you know that I love you." Jesus said to him, "Feed my sheep.**

One argument I hear among Christians is "once saved, always saved." The flip side to that is that we can lose our salvation. I am on the side of "once saved, always saved." Why? Being a dad. I love my kids no matter what, all the time. This is especially true when they screw up, regardless of how bad the screw up is. I never stop loving them. As a child of God, I believe God gives us that same love unconditionally. Once you are His child; not being His child any longer is not an option.

The perfect example of this in the Bible is Peter. Think about this: Peter denied Christ three times. The final time he did so to Jesus's face. Yet after Christ died and rose from the dead, whom did Jesus come back to and talk about love? The answer is Peter.

Why is that?

I believe it is because of the unconditional love Jesus had for Peter. He wanted Peter to know that no matter how much he denied Him, Jesus was always going to love Peter no matter what, regardless of how badly Peter screwed up. In other words, he would never leave him nor forsake him. It was Jesus's way of showing Peter, who believed in Jesus, that he was once and always saved.

It still does not take away the fact that it was Jesus who was really hurt by all of this. It was Jesus who had his feelings hurt and heart crushed by a friend denying him. Yet, it was Jesus who took the first step to mend a relationship with a friend that he had always loved and would always love.

*Just JESUS Them*

Who is in your life that you need to turn to and mend a relationship? Even if you felt the other person turned their back on you, who is it you need to reach out to and show them that they are still loved by you?

Will this be easy? The answer to this is most likely "no."

The example from today is one of the most eternal, loving and gracious acts you will find anywhere in the Bible. There were no conditions. It was a choice Jesus made, and followed through on to make sure Peter knew he was worth the love Jesus had poured into him.

*JESUSing moment>>> This may be a very difficult moment. It will also be a very telling one. You may not have any deeply wounded relationships. But you may have one or more that need a little mending. For those that have a deep-seated relationship that needs mending, go and read the entire account of Peter and Jesus (John 18:15–18; John 21). Then decide if you can Jesus them just as Jesus did Peter.*

*www.PocketFullOfFaith.com*

## Day 12
*Scratching a back.*

---

Your JESUSing Moment                                    Date

**Matthew 10:42 (The Message) *Give a cool cup of water to someone who is thirsty, for instance. The smallest act of giving or receiving makes you a true apprentice. You won't lose out on a thing.***

One task that is not very popular for pastors is hospital visits. You either like them, or you do not. They have never bothered me, other than you have no idea what you are about to walk into. There is an anxious moment right before getting to the hospital room where you are not sure of the condition of the person you are visiting. You have to prepare yourself for whatever is behind the curtain or the closed door.

On one such visit, I was not sure of the room number of the person I was visiting, whose name was Nicole. I asked for the room number at the nurses' station, and it happened to be directly behind me. As I turned to look into the room, Nicole locked eyes with me, and immediately waved me into the room.

The last time I had seen her was in another hospital and had prayed over her while she lay unconscious. To see her in her current condition was a shock to say the least. Our visit was a great one filled with laughter, talking about faith, where she had been in her health, family, and friends. It was a wonderful visit. After praying with Nicole, I was about to leave when she stopped me and said, "Can I ask you a question?" I said, "Sure" when she dropped this bombshell on me: "Would you scratch my back?" I have to be honest; it stopped me in my tracks. She pointed to the table that housed many items. One of these was a longer wooden object. I picked it up to inspect it and found it was a back scratcher.

She leaned forward and for the next few minutes I scratched spot after spot on her back. Over and over she apologized and then thanked me. There were spots she just could not reach. My

JESUS-ing moment was not the one I expected. But, for Nicole, it made her day and brought her comfort. We both still laugh about it to this day.

I know this seemed like an odd story of how to love someone, but if you asked Nicole, she would tell you it was absolutely an "I JESUS You" moment. For me, it has prepared me to expect the unexpected when I visit hospitals and get ready to walk behind the curtain or the closed door.

*JESUSing moment>>> The moral of this story is to expect the unexpected, and be prepared for it! You never know when a moment might arise that someone needs cared for in a way you will least expect. If you are going to choose to JESUS someone, expect those moments. Embrace them. Those small moments for you can be huge for the person you choose to JESUS.*

www.PocketFullOfFaith.com

## Day 13
*Following directions.*

---

*Your JESUSing Moment*       *Date*

**1 John 4:8 (NIV) Whoever does not love does not know God, because God is love.**

I am going to share with you today a little exercise you can try from the Bible. It is an easy way to get your mind thinking and it will be an easier way to JESUS someone at some point in your day.

At the end of every wedding I officiate, I read from 1 Corinthians chapter 13. The reason for this is that I can give them all the advice in the world, but God's words trump anything I have to say. I think you will see what I mean shortly. 1 Corinthians 13 is known as 'the love chapter.' Here is an abbreviated version (taken from The Message):

- Love never gives up.
- Love cares more for others than for self.
- Love doesn't want what it doesn't have.
- Love doesn't strut.
- Love doesn't have a swelled head.
- Love doesn't force itself on others.
- Love isn't "me first."
- Love doesn't fly off the handle.
- Love doesn't keep score of the sins of others.
- Love doesn't revel when others grovel.
- Love takes pleasure in the flowering of truth.
- Love puts up with anything.
- Love trusts always.
- Love always looks for the best.
- Love never looks back.
- Love keeps going to the end.
- Love never dies.

*Just JESUS Them*

If love is all of these things, then God is all of these things. Go back and read through that list. This time, replace "Love" with "Jesus."

Do you believe Jesus was all of these things?

Now go back and replace "Love" with your name.

Are you all of these things? Are you some of these things? Are you *any* of these things?

If you want to get to know God more closely, now you know what you need to work on from what you just read. It is not about you. It is about love. What part of love do you need to work on today?

**JESUSing moment>>> Share this exercise with a friend. Have them read today's devotional and try that for themselves. Then discuss it with them. What a simple way to talk about your faith and JESUS someone!**

www.PocketFullOfFaith.com

## Day 14

*Just another reminder to spend some time with JESUS as you reflect on the week, from Proverbs 3:3 (NIV): Let love and faithfulness never leave you; bind them around your neck, write them on the tablet of your heart.*

*Just JESUS Them*

*www.PocketFullOfFaith.com*

*Just JESUS Them*

# Day 15
*Watching a movie.*

---

Your JESUSing Moment                                                    Date

**Luke 2:16-19 (NKJV)** ***And they came with haste and found Mary and Joseph, and the Babe lying in a manger ... And all those who heard it marveled at those things which were told them by the shepherds. But Mary kept all these things and pondered them in her heart.***

If you have never taken the time to read the Five Love Languages by Gary Chapman, it is an excellent read. It is eye opening and very easy to learn and apply. It is also written for multiple age groups, covering adults, teenagers and children. One of the five love languages is quality time. This can be done in many forms and can involve a lot or very little activity. It can be as simple as sitting on a porch swing or taking a walk. A former student from my youth ministry, Stefan, was a quality time kid. He loved watching movies. He also happened to be the son of our lead pastor. I was his youth leader for middle and high school and he loved coming to our house to hang out with us in the summer. His dad would never turn on the air conditioning and our house was an icebox so for some reason he wanted to be with our family, especially when the temperature went past 80 degrees outside.

It just so happened that his dad preached a message one Sunday about the movies we watched. Part of what he shared was the ratings of the movies. He challenged us to stay away from rated "R" movies (and worse) due to the reasons they would be rated "R"—with nudity and language being the main culprits. Stefan just happened to spend the night at our house the night before this message. He left his bag at our house so Dallas, his dad and my pastor, was going to stop by to pick it up after church. When he stopped by the house we talked some about the message and the night before hanging out with Stefan. I told him how all we did was watch movies together. It was fun and we enjoyed that time together. I saw Dallas look over toward the cases of the movies we

*Just JESUS Them*

had rented. He smiled and said that it sounded like we had fun. He turned and grabbed Stefan's bag and headed home. Heading back to the entertainment area, I noticed that the movies he had glanced at and cringed. They were all rated "R." My heart sunk as I thought about the lesson from that day.

What Dallas did not know, and I did not volunteer, is that Stefan had picked out all of the movies. They were considered "scary" movies, and most movies that were scary like this were rated "R" due to the blood and gore associated with this type of movie.

I had screwed up completely.

At the same time, Stefan, my wife, and I hung out and watched movies together. We did very little else, other than eating snacks and jumping every now and then from parts that freaked us out. The time together was invested well and we still talk about those times to this day.

**JESUSing moment>>> *Quality time is a huge love language for many. It does not have to be a big deal or cost a lot of money. Challenge yourself to spend some time with someone today.***

*www.PocketFullOfFaith.com*

## Day 16
*Breaking bread together.*

---

Your JESUSing Moment            Date

**Luke 22:15 (NIV) *And Jesus said to them, "I have eagerly desired to eat this Passover with you before I suffer."***

Sitting across the table from me was Stan, a gentleman I had known for years. We first met as coaches for a local travel team, although we coached different age groups. We met again at the church where I became the lead pastor and Stan was in one of the churches' ministries.

Times had changed drastically since then. Our kids were no longer the bright-eyed, filled-with-hope youngsters who thought they would be major leaguers. Neither of us were head coaches any longer. We reminisced on this shortly, before moving to the real reason we were at the table this day: Stan's wife wanted a separation. She had already talked to a lawyer and was ready to meet one-on-one with Stan to discuss the next steps.

This discussion is one I have had too many times. It was the first one for Stan. He was seeking direction and needed help and hope. How to JESUS someone in this case is a tough one. What do you share with someone knowing the road they are travelling? This is especially difficult when you cannot speak for his or her spouse, who may have no intention nor desire to travel that same road to restoration. I have found over time that people shy away from these conversations. I do not care for them, either, but this is a time when a person needs actual human interaction. You, too, may be afraid of this conversation; however, here are some steps you can take to try and help him or her:

- First, instruct the couple to purposefully drop the word divorce or disillusionment from their vocabulary. Seriously—if both sides agree to this, it is no longer an option, and does not get to be part of ANY discussion.

- Get to a Christian Counselor and commit to going together for at LEAST one year! NO LESS—NO compromises.
- Remind them that in the end, each spouse involved can only work on one another individually, and they choose what they put into it.
- Relationships are NOT 50/50. Each person has to give 100/100 or they are not REALLY trying, are they?

Ultimately, the couple has to make the decision to move forward together. They also need to understand that their focus is on their devotion to one another. If they get that back, the marriage/relationship will follow.

*JESUSing moment>>> At the end of the day, what each person who is in this situation needs the most is to know that someone cares and that someone will listen. That is usually what they are NOT getting from their spouse. Just Jesus them, but focus on the restoration of the covenant they made before God!*

www.PocketFullOfFaith.com

*Just JESUS Them*

# Day 17
*Dealing with death.*

---

*Your JESUSing Moment*                                                        *Date*

**John 11: 32–33 (The Voice) Mary approached Jesus, saw Him, and fell at His feet. Mary: Lord, if only You had been here, my brother would still be alive. When Jesus saw Mary's profound grief and the moaning and weeping of her companions, He was deeply moved by their pain in His spirit and was intensely troubled.**

My wife and I were having a conversation one day when she offered this reminder: "Two things that are certain in this life: death and taxes." I am not sure I have ever received a phone call about taxes. I have received more than I can count when it comes to death.

Recently, a former co-worker passed away unexpectedly. His wife and kids were coming home from a trip out of state. When they entered the house they had recently purchased, they found him motionless on the floor. He had passed away the night before and no one was there. Imagine the horror they must have felt when they first saw him. Now imagine the guilt that surely followed knowing they were not there to help.

It does not stop there for the family. There is so much more they have to deal with in the ensuing days and weeks. It is difficult to understand until you are in this situation. Yet, when friends and co-workers hear a story of someone dying, their reaction can be all over the map. Quite frankly, many people don't know how to react when it comes death. They shut down. They don't want to face it. They pretend it isn't happening. Or, they push it aside and just move on with their lives. What they do not realize is that one day they, too, will be in that situation. It is not a question of "if"; it is a question of "when". It will happen—be certain of it. No one I have ever met has gotten out of this place we live alive.

When people are dealing with death, they need the love of others the most. They need to know we care. Even if we cannot stand the thought of seeing a friend or family member who has passed away, reaching out to those who are still here is key. It could be something as simple as reaching out with a card or a call to let them know their family is in your thoughts and prayers.

At every funeral I officiate, I speak to the friends of the family of the person who has passed away. I challenge them to take the time to reach out to the family weeks, months, and even years after the death of a loved one. It is something so small on our end but it can mean the world to the person receiving it.

Death is a difficult discussion. We want to believe we are immortal. None of us really consider the time or day that will be our last. That is why we need to hold on to the moments we have and make the most of them. Because one thing is certain: death.

*JESUSing moment>>>. Be ready to deal with death. Prepare to one day—possibly this day—to reach out to someone who has lost a loved one. What seems so insignificant to you can mean the world to them at this time.*

www.PocketFullOfFaith.com

*Just JESUS Them*

# Day 18
*Reading a love letter.*

---
Your JESUSing Moment                                           Date

**Hebrews 10:24-25 (NIV) And let us consider how we may spur one another on toward love and good deeds, not giving up meeting together, as some are in the habit of doing, but encouraging one another—and all the more as you see the Day approaching.**

Each year the two most attended services for any church are Christmas and Easter. I remember when I was younger seeing classmates and friends at these special services and thinking to myself "I didn't know they went to church here." As a pastor, we even have a term for the people who show up to Christmas and Easter services each year: "Chreasters." If Christmas and Easter are numbers one and two in church attendance every year, what would be your guess as to the third most attended service?

The answer? Mother's Day.

Why? If you ask a mom what she would want for Mother's Day, most moms want their family to be with them on this special day. Many mothers are the faith leaders in their homes. Going to church with their family would be a great start to the day for most moms.

In contrast, one of the LEAST attended church services every year is Father's Day. If you ask most dads what they would like to do with their special day, the answer is usually about them: sleep in, go fishing, go hunting, golfing, "all of the above," etc.

How sad is it that we have a God who is relational, yet most men are not? We have the right and the opportunity to call God our Heavenly Father, yet many times ignore the two-way road that is (or could be) an eternal relationship.

Regardless of what time of year it is, *weekly* church services need to be vital in our lives. If you are not growing relationships there, regardless of your age, where are you building lasting, loving relationships? If you desire to know God more personally, how can you do this when you never hear what he has written *to you?* It certainly is not something that can grow in two, or maybe three, one hour services a year.

*JESUSing moment>>> Too often, people see church as a rule-making, Bible thumping, make-people-feel-badly-about-themselves kind of place. The church is not the building. It is the people! Challenge yourself to grow lasting relationships and be a part of a church family that you not only can go, but also grow. That way you can build a relationship with God, and with others that God sends into your life!*

*www.PocketFullOfFaith.com*

*Just JESUS Them*

# Day 19

*Picking up the phone.*

---

*Your JESUSing Moment*                                                               *Date*

**Romans 10:13 (NIV) For, "Everyone who calls on the name of the Lord will be saved."**

The more that technology advances, the less personal we all get. It is easier to send a text, tweet, or post something on social media. There is little action in taking these steps (although they can be effective) causing even less *inter*action.

I lived this first hand recently with my son, Chandler, who was 18 at the time. He had to make a phone call to set up an appointment at the doctor. In the past, my wife or I had always made that call. For whatever reason, we were way past busy that day. So, I gave him the phone number to the doctor's office to make the appointment as I was heading out the door. The look on his face was what I would expect. Actually, it was what I would expect if he were donating a kidney or a lung. He looked as if he was in shock.

I told him a second time to make the call, and went about my day. When I returned home, Chandler was in the same spot, but had yet to actually pick up the phone, dial the number, and speak to another human being (this is the process for everyone who makes phone calls). He was waiting for his mom to come home to do it for him.

It was my turn to be in shock. What was the big deal? Why not pick up the phone and just get it done? He did not because we had always done it, and, in turn, had taught him how to become even more impersonal. Sadly, this is our society. This is what we have become. This phenomenon is getting worse, not better. Challenge yourself today to make a dreaded phone call.

*Just JESUS Them*

Start easy.

Call someone you really like and who is easy to talk to. Or call someone you know will not want to talk for an extended period of time.

Either way, break the barrier and the angst and pick up the phone and Jesus someone with a phone call. Here is that process again for those who are still in shock over this JESUSing moment:

Pick up the phone.

Dial the number.

Speak to the person on the other end.

***JESUSing moment>>> I realize I may have taken some liberty with today's verse. Ok, I took all kinds of liberties with it. The intent was that you will remember this verse, and that you will remember that there is still value in picking up the phone and actually using it to speak to someone.***

www.PocketFullOfFaith.com

*Just JESUS Them*

# Day 20

*Giving money to a homeless person.*

---

Your JESUSing Moment                                                    Date

**John 13:34 (NLT) So now I am giving you a new commandment: Love each other. Just as I have loved you, you should love each other.**

I live in Akron, Ohio. One thing you often find is a homeless person holding a cardboard sign at the end of off ramps or busy intersections. It is very difficult to see. There is something that triggers inside of me, personally, and questions arise.

*"What happened to this person?" "Why can't they work?" "Are they really homeless?"*

All of these are fair questions, but God did not call us to stop at these questions and drive on when the light turns green. He called us to love others *as* He loves us.

Sadly, the questions do not stop there. They usually lead to another set of questions:

*"Where will they use this money?" "Will they waste it on drugs?" "Are they going to head to the bar next?"*

Here is another follow-up question: *"Does that really matter?"* Our job is to LOVE others AS Christ loves us. Part of that means meeting people in their times of need. It does not say anything about how clean they are, how rough their lives have been, or what they will do with the things you give them.

Love others. JESUS others.

Another important part about what Jesus said is that *this is not* a suggestion. It is a commandment. It is part of our calling. It was part of his calling. It is also what Jesus did for us. If you look at the verse a little closer, you will see that it comes with a disclaimer. Part two of Jesus' command says "Just as I have loved you." In other words, we are to be Jesus to those without a home. We are to be Jesus to those without food. We are to be Jesus to those without water.

We are to be Jesus to those whose lives have been shattered. We are to be Jesus to those whose lives are shared on a cardboard sign. Without question, but always done with love.

*JESUSing moment>>> Every time I get to the end of an on/off ramp, I have no problem reaching out to those in need. It is a choice to reach out to people. I see it as God has blessed me to have an extra dollar or two sitting in my car. Prepare now and put a few dollars aside to reach others and to know what churches have food pantries and church services to help a homeless person get acclimated to that specific church until they can be part of the larger church family. Take the first step by reaching out to them!*

www.PocketFullOfFaith.com

## Day 21

How is this for summing up the week: In Deuteronomy 27:7-8 (NLV): "Give peace gifts and eat there. And be full of joy before the Lord your God. Write all the words of this Law on the stones. Make it easy to read." Your turn!

_____

_____

_____

_____

_____

_____

_____

_____

_____

_____

_____

_____

_____

_____

_____

_____

*Just JESUS Them*

www.PocketFullOfFaith.com

## Day 22
*Reaching someone who has lost his or her 'Way.'*

---

Your JESUSing Moment                                                 Date

**James 4:8 (NKJV) Draw near to God and He will draw near to you.**

Have you ever run into an old friend or acquaintance and thought, "what happened to *them?*" This happened to me recently. I was getting ice cream with my family at a local establishment. We were eating on the sidewalk when my son said to me "be ready." I asked him what he meant and his response was "you'll see."

I turned and made eye contact with a man I hadn't seen in years. We first met at an altar call almost 20 years previous. His life was a mess and he was finally ready to quit trying it on his own and give it all to God. Since that time, he had "been on" and "fallen off" the wagon many times. His marriage was continually on again/off again. His kids were in and out of trouble. His faith was strong at times, and wavering many others.

Not seeing him for years meant his walk was in trouble. Once again, he had lost his way.

I said hello to him as he walked by me. He was with a woman who was not his wife. (I actually don't know if he is married any longer.) His eyes made contact with mine, and I could tell he was uncomfortable. He covered it up by saying hello and continued on with his conversation with the woman. He didn't stop to make any introductions. After he got his ice cream, he chose to leave a different way to avoid any further awkward moments.

It will just be a matter of time before he resurfaces. He will contact someone I know, or someone within the church, and the process will start over: "I messed up. I need God. I will pray. I will find God. I will focus on my faith. I will go to church. I will join a Bible study. I will say the right things. I will read the right books. I will be a better spouse, parent, and person."

Sooner or later the next part of the process will begin: "I will compromise. I will turn away from all the things that are keeping me being a better spouse, parent, and person. I will blame others. I will blame things. It will be someone or something else's fault. I will forget about God. I will forget about the people in my life that love me and want to help me. I will stop attending Bible Study and church. My Bible will collect dust."

Repeat. Repeat again. Repeat again and again.

Or, draw close to God; take accountability and live process one only. You choose. You move. God doesn't have to. He has been in the same spot the entire time.

**JESUSing moment>>> *All of us know someone who has gone back and forth in these processes. Let's Jesus someone and grab ahold of this promise from God—even if we need to do that for ourselves!***

*www.PocketFullOfFaith.com*

## Day 23
*Sending a card or note.*

---

Your JESUSing Moment                                              Date

**Proverbs 7:3 (NIV) Bind them on your fingers; write them on the tablet of your heart.**

How do you feel when you get a handwritten letter or card in the mail? Not junk mail, or something with your name typed on the front, but an actual handwritten envelope with YOUR NAME on it? (I realize some companies are now trying to copy this by making it seem personal—so be prepared to make note of those and for getting your hopes up only to crush you with their latest "personal" offer "just for you" that also goes out to millions of others.)

Each day we go to the mailbox to get whatever it is that people who have our information are going to send us. When your kids hit the high school years, you will dread the mailbox because of all the colleges that reach out to your kids. You will also be amazed at how many schools of higher education there are. When you get this mail, you can't help but shake your head and wonder if these companies and schools know how many trees they are killing.

When you are going through the seemingly endless pieces of paper and you get to one that is hand-written, that moment can change your entire day. Some days it never comes. But, on those special days when it does show up, it stops you in your tracks and gets your heart racing.

If you are anything like me, you try to see if you recognize the handwriting. If/when that doesn't work, the next step is to look at the return address to see if who sent it. If there is no name, trying to figure out the return address is the next step in this mini-adventure. Finally, when all else fails, the ripping-it-open-to-see-who-took-the-time-to-write-you-something phase engages. This is the best part.

*Just JESUS Them*

We have a family friend who occasionally makes our day with cards. The amazing thing is, she watches out for all of us. She sends cards for birthdays, graduations, anniversaries, college signings, and even one for my wife when she got her first job as a teacher! I have no idea how she finds out these things take place.

Yet, in a world where social medial and electronic mail is king, she stops whatever it is she is doing, picks up a pen, and writes a personal note to one of us. Then she does the same on an envelope, places a stamp on it, and puts it in the snail mail. Very soon after, it arrives at its destination and the excitement begins.

EVERY time we get one of these cards or letters, we are very thankful. We are blessed. We are JESUSed.

*JESUSing moment>>> When was the last time you sat down, picked up a pen, wrote a note of encouragement or appreciation, or noted a special occasion? Follow the process above and watch what God does with that moment!*

www.PocketFullOfFaith.com

## Day 24
*Playing through pain.*

---

*Your JESUSing Moment*         *Date*

**John 16:33 (NLT) I have told you all this so that you may have peace in me. Here on earth you will have many trials and sorrows. But take heart, because I have overcome the world."**

Every family has their "thing." It may be camping, being outdoors, music, plays, or some other form of activity. For our family, that "thing" is baseball. All four of our kids play (as a note, technically Becca's "thing" is softball, but you get the idea).

For the most part, my kids have been injury-free throughout their careers. They have had bumps and bruises along the way, though. Knees hurt, muscles get sore, and an occasional wayward pitch will leave a mark on anyone. Including Becca.

Becca broke a finger the first play of her first game when she was nine. She cried for a little bit. Then her coach asked her the all-important question: "Are you hurt, or are you injured?" Becca played through the rest of the game—and had two hits! She learned an important lesson that day, as well. There is a difference between the two.

What is the difference? It is simple, actually. If you are hurt, you can play through it. If you are injured, you have to come out of the game (or in Becca's case, fight through the game, and then take time off after it!). Being injured means you may not only miss that game, but others after it. You could be out for an extended period of time.

This is the same in life. There is so much pain involved at times, that we all have to make the decision on whether or not we can continue to go through the pain day-by-day, or if we truly need to take a break and recover. This could mean a day of reading a book, taking a long drive, going somewhere to decompress, or even taking a vacation. Jesus said it best when he said that in this life we *"will* have *many* trials and sorrows." Some versions say troubles. Others say strife. Being a believer does not give us a pass. It is part of life, and you, too, have to make a decision every day, depending on the struggle.

Am I hurt? Or, am I injured?

Can I fight through this? Or, do I need to take some time off; rest in my walk, in the Lord, in prayer, in solitude, or with loved ones until I am ready to get back into the game of life?

***JESUSing moment>>> Who do you know in your life that is hurt or injured? If you are hurt, how are fighting through it? Can you share and help someone else who may be hurting right now? If you are injured (or know someone who is injured), know that it is ok to take some time off to heal. Also know that there WILL be a time that you need to get back into the game.***

www.PocketFullOfFaith.com

*Just JESUS Them*

# Day 25
*Making time to pray.*

---

*Your JESUSing Moment*  Date

**Ephesians 6:18 (NLT) Pray in the Spirit at all times and in all occasions. Stay alert and be persistent in your prayers for all believers everywhere.**

I would love to tell you that "making time to pray" was a strong suit of mine. Most people are convinced that as a leader of a church that means I have everything together. I do morning devotionals starting before the sun comes up. When the sun rises I am in silent and fervent prayer. Throughout the day I steal away to have moments alone with God. At night I tuck my kids into bed and pray with them, then go into my own room to pray before going to sleep, only to start the process again the next morning before the sun rises again.

The truth is, I do a poor job at most of this. Don't get me wrong; I feel that throughout the day I seek to recognize God in many moments. When the Bible says to pray at all times and in all occasions, Paul is telling us to seek God in each and every opportunity. God is not telling us to pull our car over at any time and get down on our knees in the median of a highway to pray. God is simply telling us to recognize who God is for WHO God is. How do we do this consistently? Here is an easy way to put this into practice. If you are a person who likes acronyms, just remember ACTS. Yes, there is a book of ACTS (short for the Acts of the Apostles Through the Power of the Holy Spirit). It is a book about the history of the church and its foundations. It is so much more. It is a book where ordinary people like you and me changed the world.

Here is how it relates to our prayer life:

In all moments **ADORE** God.
In each struggle **CONFESS** to God.
At all times give **THANKS** to God.
And always, always, always **SEEK** God.

Just like the apostles, it started with recognizing God. It continued with waiting on the Holy Spirit to fill them. The movement continued, and still continues today with people who are willing to talk to God and follow wherever He is leading. This is something we all desire. If this is your desire, as well, remember, it starts with a little prayer. It starts with recognizing God in the moment. It continues throughout the day.

Each day. Every Day. Making time to pray.

***JESUSing moment>>> MAKING time to pray is different than TAKING time to pray. When you MAKE the time to do anything, you are recognizing the need and importance. MAKE time to pray today and continue to see Jesus moment after moment, and watch Him come alive throughout each and every day.***

www.PocketFullOfFaith.com

*Just JESUS Them*

# Day 26
*Visiting a friend.*

---

*Your JESUSing Moment*                           *Date*

**Isaiah 55:8 (NIV) "For my thoughts are not your thoughts, neither are your ways my ways," declares the LORD.**

Making a visit to a nursing home can be scary for some. It is not my favorite thing to do, but I get past the anxiousness when I think about being older myself and having no loved ones around me. I would want someone to come and visit.

One person I never felt anxious about going to see was my friend Shirley. The first time I ever went to see Shirley was at her house. She was 92 years young and she wanted me to eat a piece of pie and talk with her. She insisted on cutting the pie and bringing it to me at the table. I visited her with a fellow ministry friend, and we were supposed to be there at noon. I felt badly because we were late and did not get there until 12:15. I apologized that we were there at the wrong time, to which she responded, "That's ok, I wasn't expecting you to be here until 6:30."

I knew from that moment on we were going to be fast friends.

A little over a year later, I found myself walking down the hall to her room in a nursing home. I had just met with the hospice nurse and she explained to me that her body was shutting down. She didn't know how much longer she had, as her liver and other organs were not functioning fully. Jaundice had set in, and her skin was turning yellow due to the issues with her organs.

I walked into the room to greet her. What I saw shocked me. The hospice nurse had prepared me to see something unexpected, so Shirley did not see that I was surprised. Her arms, face, and everywhere her skin was visible looked like it had been covered with yellow mustard. I greeted her with "Hi, Shirley." Her greeting back shocked me. "There you are! I have been worried about you," Shirley said. Needless to say, I was taken aback.

*Just JESUS Them*

Here was a now 93-year-old woman preparing to be with God, yet she was worried about her pastor who was less than half her age. She could see the surprise on my face at this point. "I think you need to go visit your dad." Shirley continued. "I think you need it and your mom and dad would love that, too."

I finished my visit and went home and told my wife what Shirley had said. My wife smiled, and we both knew what the next step to take was. I was on a plane in a couple of days with my son Jacob going to visit my parents.

You may have the fear of visiting an elderly person. You may never know what you might miss by NOT making that visit.

**JESUSing moment>>> Make a visit to an elderly person. Just be kind and be ready to listen. Ask questions about their lives and learn from their wisdom. Give them a view of Jesus through you as you make time for them today!**

www.PocketFullOfFaith.com

*Just JESUS Them*

# Day 27
*Bringing fairness to life.*

---

Your JESUSing Moment                                    Date

**1Thessalonians 5:16-18 (NIV) "Be joyful always; pray continually; give thanks in all circumstances, for this is God's will for you in Christ Jesus."**

My dad struggled in life with many illnesses. For as long as I had known, he had battled Crohn's Disease, which affected his intestines and digestive system. He entered the U.S. Navy at 191 pounds and at one point was down to 119 pounds due to this debilitating disease to which, to this day, there is no cure.

Because he also had Emphysema, my mom and dad were forced to move from Ohio to New Mexico. The climate there was much dryer, allowing my dad to breathe easier as he did not have to deal with all of the humidity with the climate change. Eventually his breathing got to the point where he had to go on oxygen. At first it was 'as needed,' but, eventually, it was throughout the night while he slept. In the end it was all day and night.

The longer he was on the oxygen, the more signs started showing up for early stages of Dementia. It got to the point where he recognized no one, other than my mom. I am not even sure he knew her, but he did respond to her as she took care of him day after day for the last few years of this life. My mom would be the first to tell you he didn't have Alzheimer's, as he was never combative with her, nor anyone for that matter. Regardless, the Dementia led to Parkinson's disease, to which, again, there is no cure. If you are scoring at home, that meant my dad had four different diseases that couldn't be cured, all happening to one person. It hardly seemed fair.

After writing that sentence, I can actually hear my dad saying these words to me: "Life's not fair." He was a man of few words. Yet, knowing this, he moved on with life every day. He got up at dawn, worked in the local factory until three P.M., came home and did whatever was needed around the house, took care of my mom

*Just JESUS Them*

and eight kids, and attended every game, every performance, and every family event.

In fact, I didn't even know he had Crohn's Disease until my sister started showing the same symptoms he had many years previous. His Emphysema didn't seem to bother him until he approached retirement age. I found out later from my mom that it had affected him greatly. He just never said anything about it.

Dad took care of the things God had blessed him with: his family, his land, and his home. He served as a deacon in the church. He sang bass in the church choir. He could have dwelled on all of the sickness. Instead he celebrated daily God's gifts to him.

***JESUSing moment>>> Life isn't fair. Instead of being upset and wallowing in what "isn't fair," why not reach out to someone who you know life is also being unfair to? Get together and do something that will lift both of your spirits and take the focus off of what does not seem fair. m***

www.PocketFullOfFaith.com

## Day 28

*Have you ever wondered where tying a string around your finger as a reminder comes from? Here is the verse. It also takes it one step further, as you will read before you journal about this week for yourself. Proverbs 7:3 (NLT): Tie them on your fingers as a reminder. Write them deep within your heart.*

*Just JESUS Them*

*www.PocketFullOfFaith.com*

*Just JESUS Them*

# Day 29
*Coaching a team.*

---

Your JESUSing Moment                                                  Date

**Matthew 28:19 (ESV) *Go therefore and make disciples of all nations, baptizing them in the name of the Father and of the Son and of the Holy Spirit,***

If you are looking to find a mission field when school is on summer break, look no further than baseball or soccer. Both of these sports are growing quickly in popularity among the youth and because of the boom, you will find tournament after tournament at a field near you. They will be played every week starting at the end of spring and throughout the summer and fall.

Where the goal is to bring the best out in the players, this cannot be said for their parents. It is an amazing phenomenon in youth sports that the competition can bring parents to act in such a way they would *never* accept their children to act. Yet, game after game and week after week, parents yell at umpires, referees, coaches, and opposing teams all in the name of their sport for one reason: to win.

As a coach, I saw this first hand years ago in the state baseball tournament. The one thing that separates our baseball team from virtually every other is that we pray and give thanks before each and every game. We do not take the gift of being able to play lightly, and it is our head coach that leads this charge and challenge to our players before our games.

In that year's state tourney, our team was leading the semifinal game halfway through it when the other team's coach stopped to huddle his parents. As our pitcher threw his first pitch of the next inning, their parents started yelling and screaming, using noise-makers, and even hitting a cowbell to try and rattle our pitcher. It just so happened that his dad, Chad, was another coach for our team. He looked at me in disbelief as he saw what the parents where trying to do to his son just to win a game. His son, and our team, was ten years old. Before Chad was about to explode, I put my arm around him and told him— "I've got this." I yelled out to his son, Clay: "Hey, Clay—just you and me, all day." (From that point on, I called Clay by this newly found nickname, and 'All-Day Clay' was born.) Clay, too, was in shock, but nodded to me. After every pitch he threw, instead of saying a word, he just looked at his dad; and me; and we did nothing but encourage him. One by one, Clay shut their batters down. The noise got softer and softer. The parents, still cranky, started to lose interest in their noise making. Eventually, we won the game going away, 10–5, and the next game, as well, to win the state title.

For us, it wasn't just about the win. It was learning the proper way to win. Our head coach, David, shared how important it was to encourage one another and stick together as a team, to be the example, and how doing this side-by-side can help any team achieve their goals. In life, we will all have moments like these. Jesus has put each of us on a mission field somewhere. It is up to us whether or not we choose to 'GO,' and it is up to us as to who we are making disciples.

**JESUSing moment>>> *Are you making disciples? Are you GOing anywhere to do so? Where is Jesus is sending you to make disciples in HIS name? GO and MAKE disciples!***

*www.PocketFullOfFaith.com*

## Day 30
*Saying nothing at all.*

---

Your JESUSing Moment                                      Date

**James 1:19 (ESV) Know this, my beloved brothers: let every person be quick to hear, slow to speak**

One of my biggest daily struggles is NOT speaking. I am used to filling the air with something, which typically means my voice. Over the years I have learned to pull back, even to the point of feeling the words getting ready to come out of my mouth and then swallowing hard on them.

If you are a talker like me, this is very difficult to do at times. Most times. OK, all the time. I have found that people who have to have the last word, people who have to add their two cents, people who always need to be right, people who need to give their opinion, etc., also struggle with this affliction.

Some of you right now that are reading this are laughing to yourself. You know someone who fits one or more of the list above and wish they, too, were reading this. Remember, this is also about you. So, before you want to call, text, or send smoke signals to the person who speaks out of turn, speaks too often, speaks too loudly, or is in every conversation, make sure that this is not first true about the person reading these words.

There in lies the issue.

When James said to be quick to hear and slow to speak, he was giving this directive to everyone. If your first instinct was to tell someone else, are you following what James is writing?

Relax for a minute. Read to the end. Mull it over a bit. Pray about it. Then go and live out a JESUSing moment.

After you have experienced that God moment, go and call the in-law, the spouse, the child, the friend, the co-worker, or whomever God put on your heart when you first read the devotional today.

*Just JESUS Them*

But first, be the one who follows what James is teaching. *THEN* share it personally with someone you love. Allow them to read this (without saying a word) and have the opportunity to live out today's devotional, as well. Finally, ask that person to share their story (JESUSing moment) with you personally.

When they do, be sure to *FIRST* take the time to listen.

*JESUSing moment>>> Who needs you to listen to them right now in your life? Who is crying out and you haven't really noticed? It is most likely someone who has shut down in your life because they can never get a word in edgewise. They have stopped calling, or stopping by to visit, or even taking the time to share their day with you. Go JESUS them and take action—in hearing their words and their hearts. You may be doing this for the first time. At least they will think so. THEN share this day with someone (ELSE) you just KNOW needs this (and that would be the rest of us!).*

www.PocketFullOfFaith.com

*Just JESUS Them*

# Day 31
*Making the most of THIS day.*

---

**Your JESUSing Moment**        Date

**Psalm 90:12 (ESV) So teach us to number our days that we may get a heart of wisdom.**

"You have three minutes until the store is closing," the woman in the parking lot said as we rushed toward the door. "No worries," I called back. "We are on a date and we are only picking out one item each!"

I was on a date with my ten-year-old daughter, Becca. We had just gone putt-putting and ate dinner, where we played "Would you rather" (You will read about this game on Day 57.) We had 30 minutes for the final part of our date. There was one problem, however, and that was the store we went to closed at 9 p.m. We knew of one store left open that we could get to and accomplish the final step of our date, and it was 27 minutes away.

Each of us had $5 to spend on each other. The idea is to run into a dollar-type discount store and buy something that reminds you of your date. (Your date can be your spouse or your child—try this—it is fun!) At that point, you have to cover up the gift and get back to your car. You can drive somewhere special and present the gift to your date, or you can do this in the parking lot of the store. We chose to present the gifts when we got home, and tell each other why we chose what we chose.

My little girl got me a small clipboard with magnets on the back that said 'To-Do List." When I asked her why, she said because you always have so much to do! She was right. (That clipboard is still on my refrigerator. It reminds me not to get so busy that I forget the important things in life.)

I am a bi-vocational pastor who runs a business and leads a church. I have coached all of my kids in multiple sports for over a decade. I attend every event in school and out of school (yes, there are times my wife and I have to split up to cover multiple events at the same time) and do as much as I can to help my wife around the house, the yard, and in the kitchen. My wife and I recently finished college degrees, as well, as all six of our family was in school full-time together.

I share this not to brag, nor to share that I am doing more, or less, than others. I share this because God blesses us in so many areas, and we tend to keep chasing and chasing, without enjoying moments within each day.

On this night, my 'to-do' was spending time with my little girl. Nothing more. Nothing less. Nothing BETTER. Make the most of every day. God gave it to you, and they have already been numbered.

What will you do with this day?

*JESUSing moment>>> Plan something you have wanted to do with that 'someone' God put on your heart as you read this. Don't start thinking about tomorrow or this weekend. Think about today and make it special. Remember, it doesn't have to cost a lot of money—or any money at all! Wisdom is the promise for this day when we choose to number it as God directs!*

*www.PocketFullOfFaith.com*

## Day 32
*Making an introduction.*

---

Your JESUSing Moment                                                    Date

**Luke 19:5–6 (ESV) And when Jesus came to the place, he looked up and said to him, "Zacchaeus, hurry and come down, for I must stay at your house today." So he hurried and came down and received him joyfully.**

"Hi, I'm Good-Looking Bob"

It was the best first line I had ever heard. It wasn't a pick up line, either. It was an introduction.

Standing together at a wedding we were officiating, Pastor Mike and myself just looked at each other and laughed. "Good-Looking Bob" was the third of the group of pastors who would soon be marrying his grandson and Pastor Mike's niece.

Here is the best part about his introduction: Bob did not look nor act like a pastor. He looked and acted like an every day kind of guy. He wasn't tall. He wasn't skinny or fat. He was not ripped or had piercings or was tatted, at least that I could see. He wasn't too loud or overly quiet. Until that moment, he blended in with the crowd.

But his introduction of himself broke the ice. It relaxed everyone. It had a confidence to it but no cockiness. It was genuine, kind, and still to this day makes me smile.

This got me thinking about Jesus. One thing you never find anywhere in the Bible is Jesus introducing himself. Some of us would say there was no need of an introduction. Everyone knew who Jesus was. That is not always true, either. You find times in the Bible, especially before his popularity had grown, that people didn't know who He was until He had helped someone or an event had taken place that only God could have done.

*Just JESUS Them*

Part of who we are is what we reflect. "Good-Looking Bob" reflected Jesus the day I first met him. Over time, others have met him and have shared the same introduction Bob made to me.

And, no, Bob isn't strikingly good-looking, yet he just can't help but be good-looking. The part of Bob that is 'good-looking' is what he is reflecting to every person he meets: Jesus.

Be kind.
Be gentle.
Be caring.
Be loving.

Why? The person on the other end may be meeting Jesus for the first time.

***JESUSing moment>>>Today you will meet someone for the first time. How will you reflect not who you are, but whose you are? Be ready to introduce yourself to show Jesus to someone you have never met and prepare for it now. Introduce yourself in such a way that someone can't help but know you JESUSed them.***

*www.PocketFullOfFaith.com*

*Just JESUS Them*

# Day 33
*Laughing to laugh.*

---

Your JESUSing Moment                                             Date

**Matthew 19:24 (NIV) Again I tell you, it is easier for a camel to go through the eye of a needle than for someone who is rich to enter the kingdom of God."**

*Will Rogers* was known as a humorist. I am assuming that means he was a funny guy. Rogers once said: *"When I die, my epitaph, or whatever you call those signs on gravestones, is going to read: 'I joked about every prominent man of my time, but I never met a man I didn't like.' I am so proud of that, I can hardly wait to die so it can be carved."*

Have you ever considered that Jesus had a sense of humor? If he were talking to us today, do you realize he could have us all rolling on the floor? Or, to put it in terms we get, 'roflmbo.' ('b' = butt, booty, or backside).

Think about it—we are attracted to people who make us laugh. We are attracted to people who keep our attention. We are attracted to people who challenge us to be better. Those who can help us look at ourselves, yet not take 'US' too seriously, but can take God, and our relationship with God, more seriously.

Jesus did that. And people kept coming. And coming. And coming.

In the end, Jesus took pride in dying so that we could all get to meet Jesus and spend time with Him one day. How do you think that time will go? I think we will laugh. I think we will smile. I think we will find that we missed Him in who He really was, and is. Have you ever had that impression of Jesus?

We are all too serious at times. We take ourselves, our roles, our families, our jobs, etc. too seriously? Why? We are not getting out of this temporary life alive. We may as well laugh a little along the way. Go laugh a little. Or laugh a lot. Enjoy part or all of the day with someone and share stories filled with love.

And laughter.

*JESUSing moment>>> Who makes you laugh? Who do you make laugh? Who can you tell stories with and spend the day with like you never missed a beat? Call them up and set a time to go and tell those stories. Love them and laugh with them like you always do when you get together. Then thank God for the blessing that this person is in your life that God has blessed you to laugh with on this day. Remember, you are the one blessing the other person, as well. Before you leave, set a date for the next time to get together to laugh a little more. We just don't laugh enough!*

www.PocketFullOfFaith.com

*Just JESUS Them*

# Day 34
*Telling a story.*

---

Your JESUSing Moment                                    Date

**Genesis 1:1 (NIV) In the beginning God created the heavens and the earth.**

"Once upon a time..."

Is there any better way to start a story? To me, "Once upon a time..." is much like "In the beginning..." When is the last time we read a "Once upon a time story? Usually this would mean you read a children's book. (When is the last time you read from the book that starts with "In the beginning..."? OK—let's not go there. Yet.)

I loved reading to my kids when they were little. More so, I loved to tell them stories. This usually started with "Daddy, can you carry me upstairs to bed?" At the end of the piggyback ride came the next question: "Daddy, will you tell me a story?" Whether it was about warriors or dinosaurs with the boys as the heroes saving mom in the end, or stories about princes and princesses and unicorns with my little girl, they all started with those famous words: "Once upon a time..."

Let the stories begin! Use magic tractors (one my little girl and I made up—it was also a time machine), mythical animals, sword fights, warriors, warrior princesses, anything to keep the mind thinking and the adventure going. One story will lead to the next. You get to finish one adventure and then go and start the next. The ending each night added to the magic that the story brought: "and tomorrow we will see how..." until that adventure ended, just waiting for a new one to begin.

How did the new adventure begin? It started, once again, with "Once upon a time..."

What happened to those times? What were you like "Once upon a time..."? How has the story unfolded since then? Have your kids grown and you long to have that time back? Are you counting the blessings that you had during those times, and readying yourself for the day new little voices will ask you to tell a story?

Finally, where is Jesus in *YOUR* story? Is He more a part of *YOUR* daily story than he was 'Once upon a time . . . '?

**JESUSing moment>>> Time to tell a story! It could be to your child, to a neighbor's child, to a family friend, a grandchild, etc. If you are a believer, you are part of the greatest story EVER told. Jesus LOVED children. Take a day where you can go and tell a story and love a child just as God did "In the beginning . . .," which was "Once upon a time . . ."**

*www.PocketFullOfFaith.com*

## Day 35

*Did you know Solomon wrote some 3,000 proverbs and 1,005 songs (1 Kings 4:32)? That is why we take the time to write! There is wisdom and there is song in your words that came from the moments you JESUSed others this week. Share them today as they become reminders tomorrow of when God was alive in you and your life.*

*Just JESUS Them*

*www.PocketFullOfFaith.com*

*Just JESUS Them*

# Day 36
*Being bold.*

---

Your JESUSing Moment Date

**2 Corinthians 10:2 (NLT) Well, I am begging you now so that when I come I won't have to be bold with those who think we act from human motives.**

"I came to say good-bye," Stefan said with tears in his eyes.

I sat there staring at him, trying to digest his words. Around me on both sides sat students from our youth group. No one moved. Everyone seemed stunned. In Stefan's hand was a handgun. It was pointing at the ground. It was not part of the normal attire for a church service.

"I have to go and make this right. I don't think I will be coming back. But I wanted to say good-bye to you first. I didn't get to say good-bye to my brother," Stefan concluded. His stare was icy, and he was serious. This was nothing like the Stefan we had come to know in our time together. No smiles, no jokes, no sarcasm. It was all gone.

Earlier that day, his stepbrother's body had been found in a local lake. The police shared with the family that he had been murdered. He had been shot in the back of the head. Stefan was sure he knew who had done it. He attended an inner-city school where gangs and guns were an every day occurrence. Stefan had been able to steer clear of all of this because of the people he chose to spend his time with every week. Part of those was the youth group he had come to say good-bye to the same evening he learned of his stepbrother's death.

"Well, before you kill someone can I have a hug?" The voice was not mine. It was Caity, who happened to be sitting next to me on the wall. She, too, was always able to find a way to laugh and smile. She was smiling, yet very serious in this moment. Stefan walked forward and she wrapped her arms around his head. The rest of the

*Just JESUS Them*

group hopped off the wall and followed suit. Stefan found himself engulfed by the arms of those who loved him. Shortly after this moment, one student started to pray for Stefan, for his family, and for God's peace through this tragedy.

At the end of the prayer the students took a step back. It was just Stefan and myself in the middle of the circle. I put my hand out and Stefan looked at it. He then looked at the gun in his hand. He shook his head, unloaded the gun, and slowly reached out and placed the gun, the cartridge full of bullets, and the last bullet that was still in the gun in my hand.

They say it takes a village to raise a child. This village was a youth group, and all they did that day was be bold enough to reach Stefan at the toughest moment in his 16 years of life. They were bold enough to Jesus him.

***JESUSing moment>>> Many times when Jesus JESUSed someone, he did so in the presence of his disciples. Who could you share this story with today that would join you to go and JESUS someone?***

www.PocketFullOfFaith.com

*Just JESUS Them*

# Day 37
*Breaking fear.*

---

Your JESUSing Moment                                            Date

**I John 4:18 (ESV) There is no fear in love, but perfect love casts out fear. For fear has to do with punishment, and whoever fears has not been perfected in love.**

One activity that my parents made sure we did every year was to take a family vacation. My dad loved camping, so many years we would spend at least a week in the area he was raised in Pennsylvania, the Laurel Highlands. We would drive the 5–6 hours during the day and arrive at the campground in the late afternoon. I loved rolling up in my sleeping bag on a cot inside of our tent that first night listening to the sounds of the nighttime. Soon my mind would wander to the next day and the paths I would travel throughout the campground and beyond.

One year was a particularly dry summer. At the end of the pond that people swam in at the park was a dam. Most of the time the water flowed over the edge to the stream below creating a waterfall. But on this day, it was dry, meaning I could walk over the dam to the other side of the stream. Late in the afternoon I ended up at this very spot. Looking across the river at the tree line, I noticed something I had somehow missed through the years. It was a path.

Being alone never bothered me much as a kid. I had no problem going in new directions and adventuring on my own, as my sisters were not exactly excited about getting dirty or hiking. I quickly went across to the other side and found a broken limb that became my walking stick. It was also my club to protect me in case there were any bears or wolves or dragons in the forest. Yes, I had a big imagination to go along with my sense of adventure. I started up the path to the top of the mountain. The further I went, the more difficult the path became. Rocks and overgrown weeds and trees made it it even more of a challenge to navigate. Eventually, I knew I would have to turn back.

*Just JESUS Them*

Looking back, I noticed one thing I hadn't before: the path I was walking really was not much of a path at all. Most of it was in my mind and I was not sure the exact way to get back to the area that I was familiar with at the campground. I was in trouble and I knew it. I was gripped with fear and could not move. Sounds that never bothered me suddenly were louder than ever. All I wanted was to be in the comfort of my campsite surrounded by my family. Instead, I was lost and alone.

So what happened next? We will get to that on a different day (Ok, tomorrow—but don't read ahead until AFTER your personal JESUSing moment!). Before we finish the story (I don't want to ruin the ending, but I lived), when was the last time you felt lost? When was the last time you were afraid? When was the last time you felt all alone?

**JESUSing moment>>> *Fear can be crippling. It can literally stop us in our tracks. Many time fear sets in when we isolate ourselves. God will always show you a path if you trust Him. Take the time today to be with people and be intentional in your thoughts, words, and actions.***

*www.PocketFullOfFaith.com*

*Just JESUS Them*

## Day 38
*Taking a step.*

---

Your JESUSing Moment                                       Date

**Acts 19:23 (NIV) *About that time there arose a great disturbance about the Way.***

When we ended yesterday I was lost, alone, and afraid. To recap, I had walked onto a path that I had never seen before. Before I knew it, I had gone too far and wasn't exactly sure where I was. By the time I had looked back, it was too late, as the path I thought I was on wasn't really a path at all. It was at this time that fear had set in and I froze. What happened next was what I think most of us would do when we are lost, alone, and afraid.

I cried.

Then I cried out for help. No one responded. I eventually got to the point of asking myself what my brother would do in this situation. When I was much younger, my brother Mark would walk with me on the paths in the campground. He taught me all kinds of things that you do not learn in school. He showed me which berries to eat and which ones to avoid. He also shared which of these would make you poop. He called these 'dingle' berries. Yes, he was a funny guy. He also took me 'snipe' hunting for the first, and last, time. I did not fall for it, at least not for more than an hour. Or two.

Standing on the side of the mountain, I could hear him saying to me "OK, stop and think for a minute. What would you do if you were in this situation? What would you do next?" That was a lot easier to answer when there was someone there who actually knew the answer. All I could think of at that time was I had gone 'up' the side of the mountain. That meant I had to go 'down' the mountain to get back. I didn't know which way to go exactly. I just knew I had to go down.

Still gripped with fear, but with my walking stick (and bear, deer, or dragon slayer) in hand, I took a step down. I took another step down. And another. And another. Soon the fear was gone as I was making progress heading to the bottom of the mountain. After what seemed like a million steps, I came to the edge of a brush line. On the other side I saw what was familiar—a river. The problem was, it was a part of the river I had never seen.

"OK, stop for a minute. What would you do if you were in this situation? What would you do next?," kept going through my mind. I knew the river was below the dam and I had yet to cross it. That meant I just needed to turn to my right and head back up the river until I came to the dam I had been to so many times in my life.

I made my way back up the river. As dusk was settling in, I was able to see the top of the dam. My heart practically jumped out of my chest as I made my way across the dried up dam and back to the camp sight. I enjoyed the campfire that night with my family. And, no, I didn't share this story with them for fear I may not be able to go out on my own again!

*JESUSing moment>>> Every issue we deal with comes down to one of two reasons: pride or fear. If JESUSing someone is difficult for you, stop for a moment and ask: "What can I do in this situation? What would I do next?" Break the fear by JESUSing others!*

www.PocketFullOfFaith.com

*Just JESUS Them*

# Day 39
*Producing fruit.*

---

Your JESUSing Moment                                  Date

***Romans 5:1–2 (NLV) Now that we have been made right with God by putting our trust in Him, we have peace with Him. It is because of what our Lord Jesus Christ did for us. By putting our trust in God, He has given us His loving-favor and has received us. We are happy for the hope we have of sharing the shining-greatness of God.***

One of the most difficult short-term mission trips I was ever a part of was after Hurricane Katrina hit Louisiana and Mississippi. Our job for this trip was simple: "Help to rebuild in any way possible." That was what the local construction foreman shared with us. The view of the church we worked with was a little different: "Help to rebuild in any way, but take the time to talk with the people you come in contact with on any given day—they have not seen or talked to many people since the hurricane. Many moved away from the area and few have come back."

The job for the crew I led was to deliver aluminum siding. It does not sound all that glamorous because it was anything but glamorous. But it was vital. It also came with its challenges. Because of the force of destruction of the hurricane, roads that were on a map before the hurricane were now ponds or small lakes. There were times that so many houses on a street had been destroyed that there was no longer a street to be seen. One stop had us deliver siding to a rock with a number painted on it. The only thing left was a foundation of a house that had once stood at the address.

Our final stop one day was the most memorable. The house we stopped at was like many others, except that the family had never left and had taken the last 10–11 months to rebuild. The process was slow, but they were getting to the point of having an inspection to approve the family to move back into the home. One of the final pieces was the siding we had delivered.

*Just JESUS Them*

As I met the family, the mother and grandmother wanted to show me what helped them get through this trying time. In their side yard was an avocado tree. For six years it had stood in this spot and never yielded any fruit. When the hurricane hit, it was the only thing left on their lot and the only thing recognizable to them. When construction started, the family was asked if they wanted the tree cut down. Their answer was no. Even though they were starting over, they wanted something to remind them of life before the hurricane. All they had was this fruitless tree.

A funny thing happened during the 10-11 months this family began to rebuild. The tree started to bear fruit. Most avocado trees bear fruit in the four to six year timeframe. Not this tree. It took it seven years to start to produce. This stubborn tree gave this family one thing they had lost: hope. It showed them that God is all-powerful and can bring life even when death seemed to be the only option.

***JESUSing moment>>> Where is it you can bring hope today? In a world longing to be loved, someone needs to know there is hope. Show that hope today.***

www.PocketFullOfFaith.com

## Day 40
*Putting your faith into action.*

---

Your JESUSing Moment                                    Date

***James 2:18 (NIV) But someone will say, "You have faith; I have deeds." Show me your faith without deeds, and I will show you my faith by my deeds.***

Years ago we were preparing for a mission trip to Mexico. I remember being a little nervous. After all, we spoke only English and the people there only spoke Spanish. Unfortunately, when I was in high school I took French.

If you have never been to Mexico, it is a place of high poverty and high wealth, with not much in between. The odd thing was seeing the two sides of people living next door to one another. So on any given road, you could have a mansion right next to a shack. Every road we drove down had the potential to awe us one moment, and break our heart the next. We were there to serve those in need, who were numerous, by bathing their children, washing their hair, and, at the end of the day provide them with food. Sometimes it was as simple as a giving a cup of cold water.

It didn't take long to figure out that we did not need to be able to speak Spanish. When you care for others and fulfill a need, people flock to you. An amazing thing also happened. The people there smiled, hugged us, and were thankful. Each day that we looked to bless others found us being blessed even more in return.

Do you know what language we all spoke? God's language. It was the language of love.

If you struggle with depression, anxiety, worry, doubt, etc. know this. All you need to do is go out and bless someone. Rake their yard, mow a lawn, take out their trash, make a meal for someone, etc. Do not look for anything in return. Just love them right where they are, and fill a need.

Then see what happens next.

The Bible says God is love. So go show someone some love. What you are really showing them is God. It is putting your faith into action.

*JESUSing moment>>> This is a reminder day. JESUSing someone involves action. Have you just been reading along day by day but doing little to show for it? The line next to the daily challenge is for you to fill in YOUR JESUSing moments. You may not fill in every day this year—but as time progresses you can go back and fill in the ones you miss. Don't miss today though! Let someone see your faith in action!*

*www.PocketFullOfFaith.com*

*Just JESUS Them*

# Day 41
*Celebrating with others.*

---

Your JESUSing Moment                      Date

**2 Samuel 6:14 (NKJV) *Then David danced before the Lord with all his might.***

Being a pastor, there are certain places that you find everyone watching you. My walk as a disciple has been a circuitous one, to say the least. I grew up in the Catholic Church. I was ordained in a Baptist Temple. I now lead a multi-denominational church.

Regardless of what church you attend or what denomination you are, when you go to a wedding where someone knows you as a pastor, people are watching. Will he go to the open bar? Will he get a beer or glass of wine? Will he raise a glass and share in a toast with everyone else?

But, my all-time favorite: Is he going to dance?

For me personally, the open bar issue is not something that causes me to struggle.

When it comes to dancing, this is an entirely different issue. Some days, you've just gotta dance. For someone like me, (and whose wife may or may not attest) I've got moves, and the dance floor calls my name when I go to a wedding receptions. (Or convenience stores. Or when the beat hits me.) At every wedding reception there is that one person who gets to the "look at me" stage when they dance. You can usually find them checking themselves out dance after dance in the mirrors that are in close proximity to the dance floor. My wife and I love to people watch. And when we find that person, we watch. Usually that is the person that goes from the bar to the dance floor and back again multiple times.

Weddings are about celebrating with everyone there, especially the wedding party. It is about a couple that has just expressed their vows before the Lord. The dancing I am referring to are the songs that everyone can take part in together. Doing the chicken, the

Hokey Pokey, the Cupid Shuffle, the Electric Slide, the Macarena and, just to keep it a religious experience, Personal Jesus, are what make these evenings special.

It is also a time to teach your children and their friends how to have fun in the right way. It is a time to teach them how to do those crazy little dances. It is a time to laugh and sing. Most of all, it is a time to be a part of a celebration with others before the Lord.

Sometimes you just gotta dance. When you do it before the Lord, do so in the right way, with all your might. Most of all do it as if no one is watching, even though you know others might be.

*JESUSing moment>>> Too many times we are afraid to take part in something because we are afraid someone is watching. People are ALWAYS watching. Take today to find a reason to celebrate. It may be dancing, singing—you will know when the time comes. CELEBRATE that you are loved by a powerful, yet, personal God.*

www.PocketFullOfFaith.com

## Day 42

**Did you know that the Lord instructed Moses, specifically, to write things down (Exodus 17)? Moses followed by handing the writings off to Joshua, so that they could pass these on to future generations and be remembered.**

www.PockctFullOfFaith.com

*Just JESUS Them*

# Day 43
*Taking back the dinner table.*

---

Your JESUSing Moment                                                    Date

**Luke 22:14–16 *(The Message)* When it was time, he sat down, all the apostles with him, and said, "You've no idea how much I have looked forward to eating this Passover meal with you before I enter my time of suffering. It's the last one I'll eat until we all eat it together in the kingdom of God."**

OK, crazy question time (I do this from time to time, so be prepared to think it over and answer the question before you move forward, please!): What is your favorite piece of furniture?

Most people would say their bed. There is nothing like sleeping in it when you have been away from home for any length of time. Others have a favorite chair or couch. Others could not live without their outdoor furniture because it means the weather is nice.

Before I tell you mine, let me ask you another question. Have you ever noticed that the older we get the more we eat out at restaurants? As a child, going to a restaurant was a HUGE deal. It was a holiday and a party all rolled into one. When the town I grew up in, Clyde, Ohio, got its first McDonalds, it felt like a national holiday. For our family, it did not mean going there for lunch or when we did not feel like cooking. McDonalds was still special occasions only.

Some of my fondest memories growing up are sitting around our dinner table at home. I cannot think of anything that jumps out to me as a good memory from my youth in a restaurant. It is difficult to tell stories, joke around, relax as you do at home, or talk about the events in life that matter.

In a restaurant my wife and I would not expect our kids to tell us about the first time they heard someone use a swear word, and our reaction to it. They would not share the details about what they learned in family living (if your kids are not old enough or

*Just JESUS Them*

you do not have children yet, this is the class on reproduction—be ready, it is coming!). I doubt they would tell us the guy or gal they were crushing on at the moment. They certainly would not share which teachers were crazy, or stories about classmates that may or may not be appropriate normally.

All of those happened around my favorite piece of furniture: the dinner table. Story after story, laugh after laugh, surprise after surprise have been shared there. There were tears at times, anger at others. There have been times of shock, awe, joy, and sadness. All of these can be shared and lived at the dinner table.

The nice thing about the dinner table is it does not always have to be about dinner, either. We use ours for playing cards and other board games. We have friends over and drink coffee and talk. We have other moments where people share life events.

All of these can be enjoyed and embraced at my favorite piece of furniture, the dinner table.

***JESUSing moment>>> It is time! Make a date and take back the dinner table. Enjoy some quality time with family or friends there. Turn everything else off and take it back!***

*www.PocketFullOfFaith.com*

*Just JESUS Them*

# Day 44
*Doing yard work.*

---

Your JESUSing Moment                                                      Date

**Matthew 28:19 (NLV) Go and make followers of all the nations.**

'Show some love Sunday' is a special day celebrated twice a year at our church (It is our 'GO' from today's verse). Groups of people show up from the church before service starts and get assignments to go and help people in the community with odd jobs. Why do we do this on a Sunday morning during church? Because we know people will be home. Sadly, close to 80 percent of communities are these days (up 10 percent from just a decade ago).

The jobs they do are not glamorous, but they are needed. They could be raking leaves, cutting down trees, painting, yard work, concrete work, etc. Our first service starts at 9 a.m. at the church, so the crews show up and we worship together, take communion together, they bring their offering, and we pray over the teams. We then send the teams out into the communities while the rest of the congregation finishes the service. They return after the second service and at some point share with us their stories.

Every year, the stories are different, yet they are the same. One gentleman, who was struggling with selfishness, shared it this way:

> "I am not a person who has a desire to go out and help others. I really don't think about it. One day there was a project to rake leaves. I don't even like to rake my own leaves. But, something was telling me to go that day. I did, and I met other guys who were like me. They didn't mind working, but they also didn't want to do a lot of talking. I found myself working that day as I would normally do, but I also found myself listening to stories, laughing, and getting to know some great people. We didn't even see most of the people whose lawns we cleared. But I

*made some friends that I can turn to and now look forward to the leaves falling this year to do it again."*

You would think that going into the communities would guarantee reaching people in the community. Some times it does. Many times, the families see us showing up and it is just another appointment to them. It is not up to us to determine how, or what, they feel when we are there. It is our job to love them, even when it can lead to frustration.

For this gentleman, and for many others, it gets him or her out of a rut and loving ourselves over others. It puts us in a situation to do what we do best, where God has given us talent, and to utilize those talents. Most of all, it puts us with other people to grow. This is what God intended. We were never meant to go at it alone. You never know when you will meet someone that sees the world the way you do—and it just might be God who helps you find that someone to walk alongside in the process.

***JESUSing moment>>> Have you ever thought about calling a friend and saying "Hey, wanna go help someone just because?" Most likely the answer is "no." Some of us fear we may get shot in the process. You will not. Probably. What if you called a friend to join you in showing some love to someone in need? Do it together and see what God shows you as you show someone a little love today!***

*www.PocketFullOfFaith.com*

*Just JESUS Them*

# Day 45
# RANDOM ACT OF KINDNESS (Part 1)

Your JESUSing Moment                                                              Date

***Psalm 10:1 (NIV) Why, Lord, do you stand far off? Why do you hide yourself in times of trouble?***

Synovial Sarcoma.

Not something that is normally talked about, and rarely heard. In fact, it has been discussed in public less than 1,000 times since it was discovered. I know this because this is the kind of cancer my friend Chad had. When the doctor's shared this with him, he was told there are less than 1,000 cases of this aggressive, soft cell cancer.

Ever.

I asked Chad how he felt when he got the call and they told him what it was. He said it was not as bad as you might think. He heard the news, and his first thought was "Don't sweat the small stuff." When he talked to his wife, Shawn, he told her the same thing. What was Shawn's response? "This is not small stuff."

She was right.

I believe there are times when we may question God. None of us understood 9/11. We question where God was when we hear stories about little children being beaten, abused or worse. Murder makes little to no sense as to how it could happen. Even a spouse cheating on their husband or wife leaves us shaking our heads—especially when one leaves and they leave their children behind. We cannot wrap our arms around these and many other situations.

Inevitably, it will lead us to ask God questions. Where were you, God? How could you let this happen? What if . . . ? In Chad's case, how about "Why me, God?"

*Just JESUS Them*

Do not think those questions did not go through Chad's head. They did. Chad knew, just as we all do, that it is not really up to us to question God. It is ok, however, to ask God questions. In the end, our willingness for him to be in control is what will allow us to move forward.

I will share more about Chad tomorrow. Before I do, one thing to know about Chad is his desire to love others with a random act of kindness. You never know when a phone call might come that will change your world. Chad performed random acts of kindness whenever he was able, knowing he had the opportunity to change others day and world for the positive.

*JESUSing moment>>> Performing random acts of kindness was a craze that took place just a short time ago. Sadly, the craze ended. One act at a time, let each of us change the world for the positive.*

www.PocketFullOfFaith.com

*Just JESUS Them*

## Day 46
## RANDOM ACT OF KINDNESS (Part 2)

---

Your JESUSing Moment                                            Date

**Psalm 10:17 (NIV) You, Lord, hear the desire of the afflicted; you encourage them, and you listen to their cry.**

Chemotherapy.

A term often heard and thoroughly misunderstood. It can be hopeful. It can also mean a last chance. Moving forward for Chad meant chemotherapy. Not just any chemotherapy, but the kind that is so invasive it is toxic. Doctors told him that he would only be able to take this type of chemo six times for the *rest of his life.* UP TO six times. Each time he would have to get his heart checked again to make sure he was healthy enough for the subsequent round.

The cancerous tumor that Chad had in his leg was so large—nearly seven inches in diameter—that, when shrunk, would leave him without a functioning lower left leg. Another part of moving forward was the only choice he had with his leg, which was to amputate it. They did so after his second round of chemo.

What was Chad's mindset? For him it was simple: "a life for a leg."

After four rounds of chemotherapy, surgery on his leg, and three months of rehab, Chad went back for his check up and the doctors were very positive. The procedures they had taken seemed to take care of the cancer. He had his new prosthetic limb. He had gone through physical therapy. He was walking on his own. He was even ready to head back to work.

After having his left leg amputated below the knee, Chad noticed some discoloration on his right shin. This was the same discoloration he had on his left leg before his first diagnosis of cancer. Chad went to get it checked out. When the results came back, his greatest fear was realized. What was to come next would test anyone's faith. Sadly, the doctors shared what he did not expect to hear.

The cancer was back.

***JESUSing moment>>> Did you know one in almost ever two males and one in almost every three females can expect to have cancer at some point in their lives? One in every four to five will pass away from it. This can stop us in our tracks or make us decide to act. This is a call to act. Randomly. With kindness. Today. By JESUSing someone.***

*www.PocketFullOfFaith.com*

*Just JESUS Them*

# Day 47
# RANDOM ACT OF KINDNESS (Part 3)

---

*Your JESUSing Moment*                                                                 Date

**Psalm 23:4 (NLT) Even when I walk through the darkest valley, I will not be afraid, for you are close beside me.**

Chad's cancer had come back. But it was no longer in his leg. It was in his lungs.

One thing all of us wish we could understand is when a person is hurting. We wish we had the right words, could say the perfect prayer, or knew someone who had the magic potion to make it all go away. When we realize we do not have any of those things, the only choice we have is to turn to "Who" we should have turned to in the first place. Why do we put God on the backburner? What makes us seek and think of so many other things before giving this to the one who loves us so deeply?

When Chad started into his new chemotherapy yesterday, I asked him how he was doing. He told me he was fearful of the new chemotherapy. I asked him why. His response? "Fear of the unknown."

Fear of the unknown can take us to depths that are so difficult to return. It can turn us inward and downward so quickly. Fear turns to doubt, which turns to a whole host of things, such as depression, anxiety, loneliness, or discouragement.

All of these are real. And all of these are more dangerous than any of us understand. Why? Because we can't touch them, so they are left to fester in our mind and in our hearts. Maybe you know someone who suffers from one or more of these.

Maybe that someone is you.
Know this: these are not of God.
Has Chad had dark times? Yes. So will we.
Has he had fear? Yes. So do we.
Has there been doubt? Absolutely. We all do.

*Just JESUS Them*

In the end, Chad knows this has been a battle far beyond what any of us can understand. His soul is safe and secure, no matter what the devil tries to tell him. Day-by-day, he reminds himself not to be afraid. Because he knows that God is right there alongside him. Chad wants to know that others are secure, as well. If you are feeling any pains or noticing anything out of the norm, he is pleading with you to get to a doctor and have them check it out or test it.

More importantly, if you are not resolved with where you are going after we check out of this temporary place, all it takes is some time to pray and ask the Lord into your heart. In return, he promises an eternity with no tears, no pain, and no sickness.

And remember, no matter how dark it seems right now, God is close beside you.

***JESUSing moment>>>** **We all have dark times. Heaven offers only light. Have you accepted the love, life, and light he brings into your life? We can only JESUS others if we know who Jesus is, and we know we are His. It starts by JESUSing the person reading this sentence.***

*www.PocketFullOfFaith.com*

*Just JESUS Them*

# Day 48
*Appreciating others.*

---

Your JESUSing Moment          Date

**Matthew 3:17 (The Voice) Voice from Heaven: 17 This is My Son, whom I love; this is the Apple of My eye; with Him I am well pleased.**

"I appreciate ya," was all I heard.

In a previous work life, I was a sales and technical trainer for a worldwide company in Northeast Ohio. As I was preparing to kick off a new class one Monday morning, a gentleman I had never met came into the room just before we were getting started. I looked up from my desk in the front of the classroom, only to find that he was talking to me.

"I appreciate ya," he said again. He was walking toward me with his hand outstretched. I shook it and asked him why he appreciated me. His answer was simple. "I appreciate ya because you're gonna invest into all these people in this room, including me. That's excitin'. And I appreciate ya," he said, grinning from ear-to-ear.

I found out that week he meant every word he said. He appreciated his time in his training because it meant he was better prepared to do his job. He appreciated the company that we both worked for because it meant he would have food on the table for his family. He appreciated the people in the room because it meant he had new people to meet and talk to and get to know.

He didn't take a moment of that week for granted.

I stopped often that week to think about this gentleman and his passion for people. I was struck by the fact he truly cared. The entire week came and I heard his greeting many times. The amazing thing was, people he came in contact with that week knew there was something extraordinary about him, as he had a way of making each of them feel special.

I was blessed to be one of those people. The amazing is, I can still hear "I appreciate ya!" to this day.

Who is it you can appreciate today? Who will you meet today for the first time that you can appreciate? Tell them when you first greet them, whether it is for the first time or someone you have known for years. It could be your boss, your spouse, your child or children, a friend, who ever. But tell them they are appreciated by you, and then tell them why.

As we come back together tomorrow, know this. "I appreciate ya!"

***JESUSing moment>>> This is pretty simple. Tell someone today you appreciate him or her. Expect them to stop and stare for a moment. If they do not ask you "Why?" (or suspect you are on something), tell them on your own why you appreciate this person God has brought into your life today, even if it is for the first time.***

*www.PocketFullOfFaith.com*

## Day 49

**Exodus 34:17 (NLV): "Write these words. For by these words I have made agreement with you and . . ."**

*Just JESUS Them*

www.PocketFullOfFaith.com

*Just JESUS Them*

# Day 50
*Finishing Third.*

---

Your JESUSing Moment                                                    Date

***John 19:26–27 (The Voice) Jesus looked to see His mother and the disciple He loved standing nearby. Jesus (to Mary, His mother): Dear woman, this is your son (motioning to the beloved disciple)! (to John, His disciple) This is now your mother. From that moment, the disciple treated her like his own mother and welcomed her into his house.***

If I asked you who your favorite football team was, you would most likely choose a pro team, your favorite college team, or possibly a local high school program. For me, it is the Northeast Ohio Silverbacks. The Silverbacks are a semi-professional football team. They are one of *thousands* of semi-pro teams across the country. Semi-pro teams consist of players who are former NFL, CFL, and Arena League players, former Division I and II college players, high school standouts, and guys who just love to play. Many of the players are hoping for a chance to get back in the game, either at the collegiate or professional level.

That is who they are, but why would they be a favorite team of mine? I do not have a child that plays or coaches for the team. I am not personally involved with the team. I have no stake in ownership.

The reason they are my favorite is quite simple. It is because of what they stand for, led by their coaching staff, trainers, and team owners. At each team huddle they come together and inevitably the team reminds each other of this. A coach or a player starts it, with "I AM," and the rest of the team responds with "THIRD."

The team has yet to lose focus of their dreams. They have continued to grow as a team, and grow individually in their walk with God. Through it all, they have grown together as a family, putting their personal goals and desires aside for the sake of their team.

*Just JESUS Them*

The team has yet to lose a game. That would make them an easy team to root for and to follow. But that is not why they are so easy to be a fan favorite. You can see the difference in their team compared to the other teams the minute they walk on the field. They are together, they are one, and you can feel that they are part of something bigger than each individual.

Even though they will finish first in their league, the fact that they are third is the true measure of this winning team. It is also a humble reminder of living in such a way that others cannot help but see a reflection of God.

"I AM . . . !!!" "THIRD!"

*JESUSing moment>>> Finish third today. Pray to God and see who he puts on your heart that you can go and reach out to—and then go do it, with the intent of not being first (God), not being second (someone else), but finishing in a distant third (you), and being at peace with it.*

www.PocketFullOfFaith.com

*Just JESUS Them*

# Day 51
*Giving a hug.*

---

Your *JESUSing* Moment                                    Date

**Ecclesiastes 3:5b (NLT)** *A time to embrace and a time to turn away.*

Maddie was seven years old when we first met. She was one of the players on the softball team I coached in my community. At the start of every practice she would run up and give me a hug and say "Hi, Coach Stahl!" She would then turn and run out to the field to warm up with her teammates. I looked forward to her greeting, as it was so sweet and kind. She worked hard at every practice and always did so with a smile.

In the first at bat of her career, Maddie approached the plate the same way she had every practice to date. She walked up with a smile, ready to give it everything she had. She promptly struck out on three pitches.

As she made her way back to the dugout, I saw something in Maddie I had never seen. She was crushed. Tears were flowing from her eyes and her steps got slower and smaller as she got closer to me. I wasn't sure how to deal with this. Having three boys to this point in my life, I had always coached baseball and it was pretty cut and dry: "There is no crying in baseball."

It was obvious that my normal response of "Suck it up and play!" was not going to work in this case. Maddie stopped at my feet with her head down and I could tell by the way her body was convulsing that she was sobbing uncontrollably. I looked to my assistant coaches for, well, assistance, and one by one they turned and walked the opposite direction. The final coaches to turn away were Maddie's step dad and real dad. While I was in shock at this moment, I also came to a realization. It was now just Maddie and me.

*Just JESUS Them*

Seeing as I was at least a foot and a half taller than her, I did the only thing that made sense. I put my hands on her shoulders and gave her a hug. At first, the uncontrollable sobbing got worse. Slowly, though, Maddie was able to compose herself to where I could talk to her. I got down on one knee so I was at her eye level. I looked into her eyes and asked her a simple question. "Did you do the best you could?" "Yes," she said, her voice quivering. "That is all I have ever asked, Maddie. Keep doing that. Sometimes it works well, sometimes it does not. I just want you to try the best you can. Deal?" She shook her head yes and threw her arms around my neck. After what seemed an eternity, she ran to the dugout, took off her helmet and traded her bat for her glove. She then turned to run to the field for defense. After a few steps, Maddie stopped, turned around, ran back to me and gave me the biggest hug her little body could muster.

She stopped, looked up at me, smiled, and told me "I'll do my best, Coach, Stahl!" "That's all I'll ever ask, Maddie." She turned and ran to her position. I smiled to myself for just a brief moment. It was time to deal with my assistant coaches.

**JESUSing moment>>> *Giving a hug is actually healing for both people. It puts us in a position that we extend our arms, which is good for our hearts, and it brings peace and comfort to the person on the other end.***

www.PocketFullOfFaith.com

*Just JESUS Them*

# Day 52
*Raising your hands.*

---

Your JESUSing Moment                                                    Date

**1 Timothy 2:8 (ESV) I desire then that in every place the men should pray, lifting holy hands without anger or quarreling;**

Growing up Catholic had good points and bad ones. This is true with any denomination. When it came to singing, we used an organ and hymnals. When the acoustic guitar entered the sanctuary, it seemed as though Hell may have actually broken loose for how people reacted. Before I married my wife, I started attending church with her at the Akron Baptist Temple. Talk about culture shock. I couldn't believe how many songs we sang in a row without a break. In a Catholic mass, you would break up the songs by kneeling or sitting for a while. There was no such break at the Temple. The first few times attending, I found myself wanting to sit after a couple of songs. I needed the rest.

A common trait both churches and denominations shared at the time was in the way they sang. Everything was very straight forward, and raising your hands was taboo. People looked at you funny, and you were immediately dubbed as either Pentecostal or Charismatic, or possibly both of these.

A local church asked to use our sanctuary once to see if the size of the auditorium was what they were looking to build. They chose a Sunday night to bring their choir, musicians, pastor, and invited the flocks of both churches. As their choir began to sing, the voices filled the auditorium. There was something different in the way their choir sang. Their church was predominantly African-American, and ours was Caucasian, but on this day there was a nice mix of the two congregations. At one point, their choir director turned and gave everyone permission to raise their hands to the Lord and to sway back and forth to the music. For those from the Baptist Temple, you would have thought he had told us we needed to donate a kidney. Many stood with their arms crossed refusing to do as they were instructed.

Being newer to the faith, I didn't know any better. So, I raised my hands. In doing so, I also felt the stares of many people and as I looked around, I could tell I was doing something that was taboo in our church. Guess what? I knew there was nothing against it in the Bible, and I continued to keep my arms raised.

At this exact moment in time is still that statement that sticks with me today. It was not what was preached nor sang, but there was a moment that I still carry with me to this day. The choir leader turned to the congregation and said "It's ok to lift your hands in the air to the Lord, *even* you, white people!" Being one of those white people, my arms never came down. I was there to worship the Lord, and was given permission by the person leading that worship to the Lord. That was enough for me.

How about you? Do you need permission to worship the Lord? Do you need to wait until Sunday, or when people have gathered for this specific purpose? Our life is meant to be a reflection, and we were made to worship. So, what are you waiting for? Raise those hands!

*JESUSing moment>>> Raise your hand if you love a loving God! Now go and lift someone else up so, they, too, can share in that same love!*

www.PocketFullOfFaith.com

*Just JESUS Them*

# Day 53
*Walking in prayer.*

---

Your JESUSing Moment                                Date

**1 Thessalonians 5:17 (NLT) Never stop praying.**

I shared earlier (Day 39) about a mission trip I was blessed to have led to the hurricane-ravaged area of Mississippi. Hurricane Katrina hit this region in 2005 and its path of destruction had no mercy. Whereas the people of Mississippi had no defense to this massive storm, the city of New Orleans lack of defense is what wreaked the most havoc to this beautiful city.

Toward the end of our trip, the team visited New Orleans. The area we visited specifically was known as the ninth ward. What we found shocked us. Here was a residential area that, when originally built, was under sea level. When Katrina found the breaches in the walls surrounding the city, the ninth ward was devastated. Imagine pouring milk into a bowl of cereal and watching the milk rise to the point it covered most of the cereal. This is what happened in the ninth ward.

We found ourselves on the streets of the ninth ward on a beautiful evening. The team was to attend a church service, but we navigated traffic better than anticipated, and showed up early to this now-barren place. Less than 10 percent of the people had returned since this massive tragedy. Some could not afford to come back. Some were afraid to come back. Others just moved on with their lives and started the next chapter.

At this moment, Todd, the leader of the mission team we had partnered with to get there, decided the best thing we could do was pray. The team agreed. We separated the team into smaller groups of six or seven people and sent the teams in opposite directions, which left the church as the central point. Five teams headed west and five teams headed east. A team was dropped off starting at the second block, then the fourth, sixth, eighth, and tenth block until all the teams were on the same road, facing the same direction.

*Just JESUS Them*

The idea was to walk down one road, turn down a street toward the church, walk one block, and walk back up the road toward the church until we reached the same street we started. My team was the furthest team on one end, and Todd's was the furthest on the other. When we got back to the church, Todd asked if anyone had the opportunity to talk with someone on his or her walk. Not one person had the opportunity. There was no one there.

The ward had turned into a ghost town.

Because of this we had a choice to make. We could stand still and wait for the service to start. Or we could join together and walk and pray for these people God loved who had lost their homes and their lives. God doesn't want us to stand still. He wants us to stand shoulder to shoulder and lift our voices to Him.

***JESUSing moment>>>** If you have never been on a prayer walk it can be very powerful. It is something you can do with a friend or on your own. It can be done as you walk the hallways of your work, your school, the sidelines at a game, or your neighborhood. You don't need to stop and kneel down or raise your voice so everyone can hear. Just walk. Take in the surroundings. Let those surroundings lead your heart to cry out to the Lord.*

*www.PocketFullOfFaith.com*

## Day 54
*Achieving Balance.*

---

Your JESUSing Moment                                          Date

**Romans 12:2 (NLV) Do not act like the sinful people of the world. Let God change your life. First of all, let Him give you a new mind. Then you will know what God wants you to do. And the things you do will be good and pleasing and perfect.**

If you are a person whose life is in utter chaos, you are not going to like this day. Sadly, you are most likely thinking about how you can fit these few minutes in to read this to get on to your busy schedule. Kids have to be somewhere at a certain time. You have to head to an appointment that cannot be canceled. You have to get gas in the car before you do anything. Did I mention there is that certain cup or cups of coffee that need consumed to even get you going on with your busy day?

(Before we move on, I would like to pause to give you this public service announcement. If the first paragraph describes you, know this: "Mr. or Mrs. Kettle, you are black." Sincerely, Mr. Pot.)

Balance is a very difficult task for many of us to achieve. When we think we will not be busy, we are. When we think things will slow down, they will not. When we hope to take a break, we are not able. When we desire to do something of meaning, we do things out of habit instead.

In the end, do you know who suffers?

God.

Whoa! You thought the answer was your spouse, your kids, or even yourself. But the real answer is this: God.

You see, as the devil keeps us so busy with every day life, we lose focus on the most important relationship of any life. That is the relationship with our creator. Because we lose sight of that relationship, every other relationship—with our spouse, our children, and other loved ones—subsequently follows.

That is why reading this book will bring what is important into focus. If you and I choose not to take action, elect not to fill out the JESUSing moment on the page and date it, how will we ever keep our focus on what Jesus intended for each of us to do daily?

***JESUSing moment>>> Try and stay focused on what the object is of this book. Most every day, the JESUSing moment ends with an 'ing.' The reason for that is to call you into action. You first have to read, then think about, and pray about what God puts on your heart for that special moment. Living it out when God places that moment on your heart takes that time from being just a thought to being a God moment.***

*www.PocketFullOfFaith.com*

*Just JESUS Them*

# Day 55
*Holding a hand.*

---

Your JESUSing Moment                                        Date

**Isaiah 41:13 (TLB) I am holding you by your right hand—I, the Lord your God—and I say to you, Don't be afraid; I am here to help you.**

When my wife and I were first married we lived in a congested neighborhood known as Firestone Park. This is a suburb of Akron, Ohio. The area of the park that we lived was very congested and there was little space between the houses. Our back yard was not really much of a back yard at all, and the former owner of our house decided to put a large double-tiered deck over the grass. The decks were not attached to the house. This worked for his family, as his children were older. We were just starting a family, however, and a fenced in yard with grass was needed for our two small sons, Chandler and Jacob, to play.

Needless to say, the decks had to go.

One weekend, I headed out with a crowbar, hammers, screwdrivers, and pliers, ready to take down each deck. What I thought would be an hour project quickly turned into all day Saturday, and when the sun had set I was still not finished. The next day was Sunday. When we returned home from church, Chandler wanted to go into the backyard.

He had his little hand wrapped around my first finger as we headed down the slight slope to his toys and the outdoor swing. I was half watching him, and half checking out my destructive prowess on the deck when Chandler suddenly let go as he tripped. He was able to catch himself before falling on his face completely. I did not say a word, as he was able to stand back up and took hold of my finger again. We started again toward our destination.

As I was realizing the deck was going to take at least one more day of work, Chandler lost his footing again and let go of my hand

*Just JESUS Them*

and caught himself. Once again I said nothing. But this time, as he reached up to grab my finger, I instead wrapped my big hand around his little one. As we walked on, I watched him walk, and saw that he was so intent on getting to his toys, that he wasn't getting his foot high enough to clear some small mounds of grass and dirt that were around some of the slate sidewalk path leading to the swing. The third time Chandler tripped, he tried to reach to catch himself. Instead he found he was swinging in the air, looking up at me. I had held onto him and he looked into my eyes. He was scared at first, then smiled and started laughing as he realized I had him and was not going to let go.

Needless to say, this turned into a game the rest of the way. The distance to the swing was not far for an adult, but to a two-year-old, it was an adventure and a hike. For Chandler, he realized that if he let his dad hold his hand, instead of the other way around, he would not have to worry about falling and getting hurt.

*JESUSing moment>>> Which way are you walking with God? Which way would be the best way to walk with the one you and I get to call our Heavenly Father? Part of this walk is to love as we are loved, but to rest in the fact that God has a hold of us at all times, even when we are about to fall and get hurt. Take today to pass that on to others!*

*www.PocketFullOfFaith.com*

## Day 56

**Joshua 18:8 (NLV):** As the men got up to go, Joshua told them, "Go and walk through the land. Write down what you find, and return to me." Know when you write these words that one day the idea is to return to them. God moment after God moment.

*Just JESUS Them*

*www.PocketFullOfFaith.com*

Just JESUS Them

# Day 57
*Asking a question.*

✓
_____  _____
Your JESUSing Moment                                    Date

***Matthew 16:15 (NIV) "But what about you?" Jesus asked. "Who do you say I am?"***

Would you rather have one arm or one leg?

Would you rather be blind or deaf?

Would you rather have all the money in the world and be terminally ill or be poor with nothing and have your health?

"Would you rather" is a game I have played for years with all kinds of people. Whether it is with my youth group, neighborhood kids, or my own children, it is always interesting to hear how people will answer these types of questions. It is even more interesting hearing their explanations as to why.

But, *every* time, the last question stops people in their tracks. It most likely did the same for you when you first read it. Or, more likely, you are going back to it and really thinking it through.

When I ask this question to younger people, their explanation is telling. They have all the money in the world so they can pay for the research to have a cure for their illness. When I explain that the illness has yet to be cured to date and it more than likely will not be cured even with all the research they pay for, they hesitate slightly. But, in the end, they always choose to take their chances on the cure.

Older people are different. When you ask this question, they choose their health. Time has shown them what the loss of a loved one means. They long to see that person's eyes, talk to them again, or be with them one last time. If they could buy that, they would use all of the money in the world to do so. Since they know they cannot, they would not trade all the money in the world for their own health. They know it is not a fair trade.

That is why asking these and other questions now bring such importance. It seems trivial, but if you look at one of the ways Jesus loved, it was through asking questions. What questions can you ask today that bring meaning? What questions can you ask that will show people how much they are loved?

One last question, and, remember, these are not to make you feel guilt but to help you extend grace to others, starting with yourself. Would you rather stop and ask questions now or wish you had taken the time to do so later?

**JESUSing moment>>> *Grab a cup of coffee or a cold drink or just sit in a room, on a porch, or while you are driving and ask questions. It sounds simple. And it is. But it shows others that you care and that they mean something to you.***

*www.PocketFullOfFaith.com*

## Day 58
*Attending calling hours or a funeral.*

---

*Your JESUSing Moment*                                                  *Date*

**Luke 9:60 (ESV) And Jesus. said to him, "Leave the dead to bury their own dead. But as for you, go and proclaim the kingdom of God."**

What is a time of life that people are most in need? Many times these moments are centered on life changing events. This could mean a celebration such as a birth of a child or a wedding. It could also mean a tragedy such as an unexpected call or a death in the family.

As a pastor, one life lesson you are taught is that every funeral is the same, and every funeral is different. In all of the funerals, someone has died and the family is burying their loved one. In every funeral, though, the person dying is different. You could have many of the same family members mourning, but no one has ever died twice.

Not one.

That is why this moment is such a huge JESUSing moment. The family and friends of the person who has died are as numb as they are going to be. They need to know others care. They need to feel loved. But they also need hope. That is why Jesus said to go and proclaim the kingdom of God in this verse. That is also why the pastor doing the funeral needs to share this hope.

That is his or her role.

What is the role of the person who is a friend or family member of the deceased? Attend the calling hours. If you are not able to attend the calling hours, attend the funeral. Be there for one, or both if you are can, but attending one means more than words can say to those who just lost a vital part of their life.

*Just JESUS Them*

If you are a person who fears death, know this: you do not have to go alone. Meet a friend, a member of your family, or someone from your church at the funeral home or church where the funeral is held. You don't have to say much. Let them know you are there and that their family is in your thoughts and prayers.

Look at the pictures. Share in the memories. More than anything, listen to those who have suffered this ultimate loss.

As for you, GO. Through going, you, too, just with your presence, can proclaim the kingdom of God.

***JESUSing moment>>>** This is one of those moments that you cannot actually plan for, but do need to be prepared. It will happen. Make sure you are ready so you can be there for a friend who has suffered a loss. Once you overcome this fear, it will get easier. You have to be prepared to take the first step and Jesus someone in this difficult time of need. You may be the only Jesus they see during this difficult time.*

www.PocketFullOfFaith.com

*Just JESUS Them*

# Day 59

*Being who God made you to be.*

---

*Your JESUSing Moment*                                        Date

***John 3:30 (NLT) He must become greater and greater, and I must become less and less.***

If I gave you someone's job position and asked you to picture that person in your head what would you come up with? Let's try this together. If I said "police officer," you would think of someone in a black or blue uniform with a badge and a gun by his or her side. If I said "doctor," you would most likely picture someone in a white lab coat with a stethoscope around his or her neck.

But what if I said pastor?

For some they would immediately think of an older gentleman with white hair and a three-piece suit. Others may picture a flashy person with gold rings but still dressed to the hilt, suit, tie, and dress shoes.

The day I met Pastor Jeff he was none of those things. I cannot tell you how refreshing that was and how relaxed the meeting and conversation was that followed. He showed up to our meeting in a flannel shirt and blue jeans. He wore sandals with no socks. Personally, it is how I believe Jesus would greet others as he walked town to town if He were with us today.

The best part about our first meeting was getting to know him a little better. It is so refreshing to find people that are "normal." He is a husband who loves to be married. He is a dad that loves to be a father. He is a worker and a friend who cares for every person He comes in contact with every day.

Jeff may not like me calling him "normal" because he is anything but that. What I found was a genuine, caring, and kind person. I found someone who was comfortable in his own skin. I also found a person with so much love for God that he wants nothing more than to show and share that love with others. It is every part of his person and it is in every part of the church he leads. If you were to ask anyone at his church what the focus of being a member at this church would be, they would all tell you the same thing: Know it, Live it, and Give it away.

In other words, Know Jesus, Live Jesus, and Give Jesus Away—it is what Jeff does every day and what he teaches those he reaches every week in his messages. It starts with him being comfortable with who he is, and whose he is.

Even though he does not wear a suit. Even though he does not wear a tie. Even though he does not wear socks. Jeff, and those he loves and serves, live and learn to Jesus others.

**JESUSing moment>>> Know it. Live it. Give it away. So simple, yet so powerful! Time for you to go and Jesus someone! Make sure to record it above, as well! You can even honor Jeff by honoring Jesus: do not wear any socks when you do so.**

*www.PocketFullOfFaith.com*

*Just JESUS Them*

# Day 60

*Listening in the living room.*

---

Your JESUSing Moment                                      Date

**James 1:22 (NIV) Do not merely listen to the word, and so deceive yourselves. Do what it says.**

I was sitting in my living room looking out our front window when a truck pulled in the driveway. My friend Mike got out of his truck and started making his way slowly to my front door. It was hard to believe, but just two short weeks before this his 17-year old son, Micheal, also known as 'Mikey," had taken his own life.

I got to the front door before Mike did. He was reaching for the doorbell as I opened the door, and I startled him. "Whoa," he said, stepping back. I laughed and immediately invited him into the house. "Were your ears ringing?" I asked Mike. "I was planning on coming to see you today as I have something for you. You beat me to the punch!"

For the next hour we talked. Mike talked mostly, and I knew that was important. When he needed my help, I would answer his questions. I am not saying I had the right answers. In death, especially suicide, I am not sure anyone does.

The talk centered mostly on his son's death. Mike was still numb. He shared with me that he wanted to see and talk to Mikey. He wanted the opportunity to see him graduate from high school; to go into the military (Mikey's plan after high school); and to get married and have kids.

All of that was gone.

Part way through our talk, I shared with him that I planned to stop by the drive thru that his family owned and ran. I was going to bring him a book that many at my church have used daily to grow. It was a book written by a man who had lost his son just as Mike had. The book is *The One Year Uncommon Life Daily Challenge* by Tony Dungy and Nathan Whitaker.

*Just JESUS Them*

I opened it to that day's date and read it to him. I could see he was thankful for it. Eventually he had to leave. I prayed with him before he left on my front porch. I gave him all I had to offer that day: an ear to listen, a book to reach him daily, and prayer.

It was all I had. To Mike, it was more than enough.

I enjoyed that time that day with Mike. I just did what I had learned through the scripture reading today: to be a doer of the word and not a hearer only.

An amazing thing happened that day, as well: I JESUSed Mike. In return for this, through our conversation and his kindness, Mike JESUSed me.

***JESUSing moment>>> Love is a verb. It is not just something we think, feel, or say. JESUSing someone is love in action. Who can you JESUS today? It could be something as simple as sitting down and listening to someone. But YOU have to take the action. As James shared in a few short words: Just DO it!***

*www.PocketFullOfFaith.com*

## Day 61
*Doing something simple.*

---

Your JESUSing Moment | Date

**Ephesians 4:15 (NLT) Instead, we will speak the truth in love, growing in every way more and more like Christ, who is the head of his body, the church.**

KISS

What do you think of when you read that word? For some it is a rock group with face paint. When I was younger KISS was going to keep their face paint on until the year 2000. Sadly, their popularity waned, and they decided to unmask themselves earlier. After doing so, many fans wanted them to put the paint back on their faces. They did. It was part of what made them KISS.

When I look at the word KISS, the acronym for Keep It Simple, Stupid comes to my mind. As a personal reminder, I change the last word and change it to Keep It Simple, Stahl. Sadly, I need this reminder often. Why? I overcomplicate things on a consistent basis.

I see this often in society, as well. Businesses have an idea to take something to market, only to get stuck when committee after committee cannot agree on the simplest of ideas, such as the date of release or the color of a package. Local youth sports organizations start with the best intentions only to see parent after parent mess things up by being ultra competitive. Some school districts push for levies and tell voters things that are not true and wonder why nothing passes when the levies are taken to the ballot.

Time after time, what started off as a simple, great idea became overcomplicated and never made it anywhere. In its wake, businesses tread water, children are left without coaches who care and/or fields to play, and people lose faith in the leadership of their schools and churches. Sadly, these are just a few examples where KISS got lost in the translation.

*Just JESUS Them*

Even sadder, this happens to us in our lives. We each have an inner desire to help others in some way. Too often, we overcomplicate helping others with meeting after meeting and person after person needing to take part. Dates get pushed back. People cannot show up at a certain time. In the end, nothing gets done nor does anyone get help. Time fades away as the KISS has worn off.

What happens to us, personally? We become jaded, angry, or turn our backs and end up doing something else. Even worse, we do nothing at all.

Time to take the mask off and get back to what made KISS great: Keep It Simple, Silly. Oh, and Keep It Savior Simple. Just Jesus Them!

***JESUSing moment>>> We taught this once as a series for our church. It started as Keep It Simple, Servant. It ended as Keep It Savior Simple. It starts by keeping it simple, one act at a time, with Jesus as the lead! Simple! Keep it that way!***

*www.PocketFullOfFaith.com*

*Just JESUS Them*

## Day 62
*Stop pretending.*

---

| Your JESUSing Moment | Date |

**Romans 12:9 (NLT) Don't just pretend to love others. Really love them. Hate what is wrong. Hold tightly to what is good.**

Nobody likes a fake. Whether it is counterfeit money, a Rolex, a purse, or shoes, we all want the original. Over the years, many professions have taken a beating when it comes to lack of integrity. Whether the job is an attorney, car sales person, working for the government, or especially, dealing with taxes, we all want the real deal.

I read a study recently where people were asked to name the most trusted professionals. Female nurses and female teachers earned the top two spots. Doctors and male nurses and male teachers fell further down the list. One profession of note that I found below both of these really hit home for me, personally: clergy.

I was meeting with a church that had three potential pastors being interviewed to take the role of lead pastor. In listening to the candidates speak; there was something off about one of the finalists. None of us could really out our finger on it, especially because it wasn't noticeable when he spoke in large group settings such as a Sunday message to the congregation. It was obvious behind closed doors, however, that the person at the pulpit and the person one-on-one were not the same person.

Thankfully, he finished third of the three candidates in the review committees voting. Sadly, the first two candidates turned down the position. He gladly accepted, and took more than 80 percent of the congregation vote. In the voting by the employees, leadership, committee, and pastors—in other words, those who had the chance to get to know him—the percentage for and against was closer to 50/50.

Years have passed since the vote took place. None of the original pastors is still on staff. The office staff has turned over and other key leadership has left for various reasons. The new clergy that was leading was only pretending to love others. The leader said the right things for a while, but eventually the true colors and the true person inside started to come to the surface.

Quick question time: when you read this devotional, do you read it to take action? If so, are you taking action? Part of our character and integrity shows when we make the choice to follow through with the plans God has for us. That means not merely listening to the Word, but doing something about it.

So, be honest with yourself. What are you doing with this daily devotional? Are you loving others as Jesus loves you? Are you actually JESUSing anyone? Are you being authentic about it? Are you just pretending and going through the motions? Remember, nobody likes a fake.

***JESUSing moment>>>** If you have been JESUSing people every day, keep at it! Be real. Be honest. Choose right over wrong. Have character and integrity while doing so. If you are just pretending and not filling out YOUR JESUSing moment with the date, what are you waiting for? Go love someone. Really love them. JESUS them!*

www.PocketFullOfFaith.com

## Day 63

Do you need a reminder as to why we write things down? Here is what Paul wrote in Romans 12:3 (NLV). It is a nice reminder as to why it is important to journal: God has given me his loving-favor. This helps me write these things to you.

*Just JESUS Them*

www.PocketFullOfFaith.com

Just JESUS Them

## Day 64
*Fearing no more.*

---

Your JESUSing Moment Date

***2 Timothy 1:7 (ESV) for God gave us a spirit not of fear but of power and love and self-control.***

Did you know the term 'be not afraid' is in the Bible 365 times? That tells me this should be a daily reminder for each of us. I know so many people that live in fear every day.

Many of these fears they have no control over, yet they consume them. They have a fear of the stock market crashing. They fear that gas prices will rise beyond their means. They fear when their children go to school. They have a fear that the weather may change drastically. They have a fear of tomorrow and what the future might hold. They literally fear everything. The sad thing about fear is it stops us in our tracks. An even sadder thing about fear is where that emotion comes from. It is not from God. In fact, it is quite the opposite.

Here is how a friend of mine, who found himself living his life in fear, described it. It was controlling him, his work, his home, and everything he did. His fear was specific as well. This fear is something many of us can relate to:

> "I had a fear of people. I am an introvert and it was tough for me to reach out. But Jesus did not hide from people. He met them right where they lived. I found myself going to an inner-city ministry in need of help. I started to volunteer and found that being an introvert was not the curse I thought it was. I am still not what people would call outgoing, but I have noticed that serving others has allowed me to come out of my shell. I have built such strong relationships with the people I served, and a crazy thing happened. We became friends. Through this, I learned that God did not intend for me to be alone or

*Just JESUS Them*

> stay alone. God is relational. God doesn't want any of us to fear others. He gives us a spirit of love. We just need to let that control us so we can love, too."

My friend's fear is a legitimate one. So common, it has a name: *Anthropophobia*. Unchecked, it can lead to isolation. It can also lead to the only communication a person with *Anthropophobia* can muster, which is social networking or other electronic means. In other words, their fear of people can lead to no longer associating with people. When people learn this, their lives can change in an instance. They are no longer crippled by that fear. Instead they find themselves going, reaching, and most of all loving others. They eventually learn that love for others is what controls them in their everyday life.

It is now your turn. No more living in fear. It is time to JESUS someone.

**JESUSing moment>>> Put down the phone. Do not use e-mail. No text messages. GO and see someone. Spend some time with a person from your church, work, neighborhood, school, team, etc. Meet them right where they are in life, and right where you are in yours. At the crossroads of where those two intersect, when we love others as Jesus did others, that is where we will find JESUS.**

*www.PocketFullOfFaith.com*

*Just JESUS Them*

# Day 65
*Experiencing JOY.*

---

Your JESUSing Moment                                       Date

**Luke 10:27 (NIV) He answered, "'Love the Lord your God with all your heart and with all your soul and with all your strength and with all your mind'; and, 'Love your neighbor as yourself.'"**

I am not sure what it is, but some people struggle living with JOY. There are some people that have to have contention and drama in their life. They complain about their job, they complain about their spouse, they complain about the communities they live in, they complain about their schools, they complain about their church.

Complain, complain, complain. It is exhausting.

If you are around someone like this, all you can do is listen. The reason for this is twofold. If you say anything you are only adding fuel to the fire. This can be difficult for reason number two. This person complains so much and so often you can never get a word in edgewise!

How do we avoid being around those who have nothing but negative things to say? How do we ensure that we will never become a person such as this? It is very simple. If you are a person who likes acronyms this is the one you need to remember and make a part of your every day life.

JOY. Jesus Others. You. What you will find with those who have nothing better to do than to complain and live with contention in their lives is that their focus is completely skewed. They only talk about themselves and only care about themselves. They have no JOY in their lives. For the rest of us, in order to live with JOY, we need to be prepared in every relationship to show and share JOY. This is what Jesus commanded us to do in today's verse. It is a very easy principle, but, sadly, rarely put into practice.

It is also a principle we *choose* to live and separate ourselves as a believer when we *choose* to live with JOY. This is a *choice* you and

*Just JESUS Them*

I make every single day. Know this: we are the ones who *choose* to live with or without JOY every day, just as those who live with contention and drama *choose* to live without JOY every day.

Which do you *choose?* I choose JOY. Jesus. Others. You.

*JESUSing moment>>> What do we do about the person who has no JOY in their life who does nothing but drag others down? We will focus on that tomorrow. First we need to choose to live with JOY before we deal with those who have no JOY. That may seem backward based on what we just read. Remember, they need to see Jesus in you before they can ever hope to live with that same JOY. We need to prepare and practice to be that JOY for others who need it and will accept it more readily. Be ready to bring JOY to whomever God brings in your life. As for those you know personally who have no JOY? Well, we will see you tomorrow!*

*www.PocketFullOfFaith.com*

*Just JESUS Them*

# Day 66
*Avoiding JOYsuckers.*

---

Your JESUSing Moment                                              Date

**Proverbs 10:20 (TLB) *When a good man speaks, he is worth listening to, but the words of fools are a dime a dozen.***

Yesterday we learned all about JOY: Jesus, Others, and You! Today, we are doing a complete 180. Have you ever been around that one person that can literally suck the life out of any situation? Here are a few examples:

- ➤ You go to a wedding to celebrate a young couple, and there is that one person who was left at the altar, engaged three times, or is just getting over their fourth marriage and they want to share all of it with anyone who will listen. Not the good times, either. ALL of the bad ones.
- ➤ You are at a birthday party for your child and all of the kids are having fun. There is that one child who will only play with one other child. When they do not get their way, they choose to do nothing at all. You do all you can to get them involved, only to find the time goes so quickly that you did not enjoy the party for your child because of this other child.
- ➤ You are having a conversation with friends when "that guy" or "that girl" walks in the room. You do everything you can to avoid any and all conversation, but they see you and your group and come to join in the discussion. They are not really joining in the discussion. They are waiting for the opportunity to jump in and change the direction of the talk. It needs to be about him or her, and he or she proceeds to take this enjoyable time and turn it into a pity party or a complaint session.

Simply put, these people are anything but the life of any party. In fact, they are the complete opposite. They have a name, too. They are "JOYsuckers." If there is any chance that anything positive, anything fun, or any bit of laughter is going on and this person comes into the room—*ffffffffffppppppphhhhhhhhhhtttttttt*—they suck all the life out of the room.

Why is this so important and being discussed in a devotional meant to JESUS others? Because people like that can take every bit of joy OUT of you, which means you have nothing left to put INTO someone else. You leave JOYsuckers feeling tired, defeated, saddened, and beaten. It could be a co-worker, fellow student, boss, neighbor, or even someone from your church! Regardless, it is time to run FROM them—and run TO someone that you can Jesus.

Until that person starts to live with JOY, they will continue to suck the JOY from anyone that will listen. Run. Do it quickly. Do it before there is nothing left in you, and you have nothing left to give of your self to others.

***JESUSing moment>>> We all know people like this. Stay away from them at all costs. All the energy you use dealing with them is energy that could be spent wisely elsewhere. Part of JESUSing others is to do so to those who WANT to be JESUSed. JOYsuckers are about one thing: themselves! Jesus was about one thing: others. Who would you rather be more about?***

*www.PocketFullOfFaith.com*

*Just JESUS Them*

# Day 67
*Donating your self.*

---

Your JESUSing Moment                                      Date

**Exodus 36:3 (TLB) Moses gave them the materials donated by the people and additional gifts were received each morning.**

The Baltimore Ravens and Pittsburgh Steelers are household names. Their battles on the football field are both brutal and legendary. The fact that the two teams play in the same division, hate one another with a passion, and would do anything to knock the other team off the pedestal only adds to their rivalry.

Ma'ake and Chris Kemoeatu are not exactly household names. They are brothers and NFL football players. The fact that one brother plays for the Ravens and one plays for the Steelers is interesting. The fact that one brother is on the defensive line and the other is on the offensive line adds more intrigue.

Sadly, Chris's career was cut short. He has been battling kidney issues since he was in middle school. The ailment got so bad during his playing days with the Steelers that he would eventually need a transplant.

Getting a kidney transplant is not like changing a tire, or a light bulb. When a kidney fails, there has to be a match in order for the body to take the new kidney and function. Chris was also 345 lbs. which was a challenge when it came to finding a match. So, who stepped in when a match was needed? You guessed it, big brother Ma'ake. The oldest of seven children, Ma'ake was taught that it was his responsibility to take care of his younger brothers and sisters.

Of course, this story has to have a twist. You see, in order to give of himself to his little brother, it first meant he would have to give up his NFL career. It meant he had to give up something he had worked so hard to achieve. The countless hours of lifting, running, and practicing, to reach his dream would all end in just a few hours of surgery.

*Just JESUS Them*

Ma'ake never gave it a second thought. Ma'ake didn't want to be in a position that he could play and his brother could not. When it came time to step up and give of him self, he knew there was no other choice. He gave freely and with no regret. If you were to ask Chris, there is something far greater that he gained. The two brothers grew even closer together through this experience. This is what happens when someone gives of himself or herself to help others.

Some people donate time. Some people donate their person. Some people donate money. Some even donate a kidney. Jesus donated his life. All of these are examples of giving something they have that can help someone of need.

Where or what is it that you can donate today to help someone in need?

*JESUSing moment>>> It could be a food bank. It could be a shelter. It could be a child in need. It could be a natural disaster. It could be pulling off the side of the road to help someone change a flat tire. Jesus donated his life for all of us. Challenge yourself to donate in some way today and JESUS someone in a way they never saw coming.*

*www.PocketFullOfFaith.com*

*Just JESUS Them*

## Day 68
*Finding Beauty.*

---

| Your JESUSing Moment | Date |
|---|---|

**Acts 3:2 (NLT) As they approached the Temple, a man lame from birth was being carried in. Each day he was put beside the Temple gate, the one called the Beautiful Gate, so he could beg from the people going into the Temple.**

I wanted to walk right past the man trimming the bushes. After all, the last three people we had talked to were doing similar jobs, and none of them could speak English. Why would I waste my time on another person that could not communicate with us?

One of the young ladies in my group, Wizzie, grabbed my arm and pointed at the man. "What about him," she asked? I tried to plead my case using the previous workers not speaking English as the example so we could move on to the next person. Wizzie pressed me. "It couldn't hurt to say something to him to at least find out if he speaks English. I mean, how much time would that take?" She made a great point. (Actually she made two.)

I guess I should explain where we were to make this a little clearer. I was leading a trip of 58 people on a mission trip in the Bahamas. Most of the people there were native Bahamians. Others were Haitian. The rest of us were on the mission trip. Begrudgingly, I walked over to the gentleman trimming the bushes. I introduced myself and asked if I could have a few minutes of his time. At first he just stared at me. I was sure that stare meant that he couldn't speak English. I was wrong. Many people know the Bahamas as a vacation area. But behind the vacation area is a culture that is very poor. They have very little. What they do have they take pride in, personally. This man was taking pride in his yard work. He told me he wanted the outside appearance to be attractive to others.

We spoke more about what our inside appearance looks like to God. We talked about having a relationship with him. He looked forward to the one day a week that a family member would come

*Just JESUS Them*

to his house and read it to him, as he was unable to read. I shared with him how much God loves us. How God sent his one and only son for each of us. That Jesus is powerful, passionate, and personal. I also shared that God loved us from the inside out. No matter what struggles, doubts, worries or anything we dealt with on a daily basis. God gave Jesus to love us just as we are.

I soon found myself with this man, Wizzie, and the others standing in a circle and praying to God that day. We prayed for this man and we prayed for his salvation. I was so busy and focused on the outside, or as the verse today says, the Beautiful Gate, that I forgot to check the inside of one man. This man was 81 years old. After accepting Christ, he looked me in the eye and said "Now I know why God has kept me here so long." With tears streaming down his face he thanked me and smiled.

The last thing I asked this man—which was normally the first thing—was his name. It was Jewel.

*JESUSing moment>>> Read today's verse again and ask yourself if you are so focused on the outside that you are forgetting the person on the inside that needs loved. What can you look past to care for a person today that needs to know they are special in God's eyes?*

www.PocketFullOfFaith.com

*Just JESUS Them*

## Day 69
*Throwing a ball.*

---

Your JESUSing Moment                                     Date

**1 Corinthians 16:14 (NIV) Do everything in love.**

We recently got a puppy. His name is '. He's a Cavachon, which is a mix between two other breeds and a smaller dog in stature. Toby weighs roughly 12 pounds. He has always had a ton of energy, although I would not consider him a hyper dog.

One game Toby loves to play is "fetch." The funny thing is that Toby will only play fetch with a ball. Rather than call it "fetch," we just call it 'playing ball.' Ever since he was a puppy you could throw a ball in the yard or in the house and he would chase it and bring it back to you. Toby would then wait for you to throw the ball.

Again. And again. And again, and again, and again.

One thing Toby does not understand is timing. When he was just a few months old, he would jump up into bed with my wife and me. He would climb on top of me and drop a ball on my chest. The ball would roll off into the crook of my neck. Toby would run off of me, around my shoulder, and grab the ball. He would then climb back onto my chest and start the process again.

Again. And again. And again, and again, and again.

Eventually I had to make a choice. I was either going to be angry at this tiny little puppy, or I was going to *have* to play ball. Needless to say there have been a lot of 3 a.m. games of 'playing ball.' Quite frankly, I really don't mind getting up to play with him. He does not talk back to me. He does not expect any more from me. He enjoys the time together. Best of all, he makes me laugh because he plays with such passion every time. His passion is contagious even to me, his human. So I play ball with him at all hours of the day and night.

Again. And again. And again, and again, and again.

*Just JESUS Them*

Since there's no one to talk to in the late hours of the night, I mean morning; I often found myself deep in thought while throwing the ball to Toby. Since I began writing this devotional, I still wonder if I am living my life as Jesus would intend? If my desire is to truly love as Jesus loves, why do I *not* treat JESUSing others as Toby does playing ball?

Simply put, Toby makes playing ball look easy. He loves the time and he loves the chase. His passion for playing ball has never waned, and it is never ending. Toby relishes in doing what God his given him a passion to do every day. Do I have that same passion to live with that same passion? Do you? Not just one day, either. Every day.

Again. And again. And again, and again, and again.

***JESUSing moment>>> I know we all have different challenges daily. If there is something you love to do that will show God's love to others, choose to do that today. Then do it! Give the credit to the Lord, and do not be afraid to share that with others. Then repeat it, daily. Again. And again. And again, and again, and again.***

www.PocketFullOfFaith.com

## Day 70

Paul once wrote in Romans 15:6 (NLV): "I am able to write these things because God made me a missionary to the people." What can you write about this week from your missionary journey?

*Just JESUS Them*

www.PocketFullOfFaith.com

# Day 71
*Taking the first step.*

---

Your JESUSing Moment                                             Date

***1 John 4:18 (NIV) Such love has no fear, because perfect love expels all fear. If we are afraid, it is for fear of punishment, and this shows that we have not fully experienced his perfect love.***

The first time I saw Gary he could barely take a step. In fact, every step he took looked painful, and it took him an eternity to walk more than 20 yards. Yet, every morning there was Gary walking down my road. An amazing thing happened with Gary. The more steps he took each morning, the smoother his walk became. Gary was a very large man. The reason he struggled walking even a few steps was due to his weight. Over time you could see the weight loss. As Gary's strength grew and the pounds started to shed one by one, he was able to walk a little easier. The easier it became, the further he was able to walk.

When he first started, breathing was difficult for him even walking to his mailbox, which was roughly 50 feet. Gary continued to walk, and the more he did so, the more he was able to get his wind. One morning I ran out to Gary. I noticed he did not have any water to drink. He laughed and told me he was good. He said he would get a drink of water when he got home. He shared with me that he drank a glass of water before he left for energy. He drank another glass of water when he got home for refreshment.

I told him my wife and I noticed him walking every day. I also told him that we could tell he was walking without the pain that was obvious when he first started. What used to look like a chore was now very fluent. Gary looked at me and thanked me for noticing. The funny thing was, he never broke stride. He just smiled to himself and kept on walking.

I believe many times this is what stops us in our walk of faith. We get so comfortable that over the time we get lazy. What used to seem so easy becomes more and more difficult. We carry the weight of our failures, struggles, and shortcomings to the point we cannot even take a step of faith. That is the main reason I started writing this book. It is to get people to step out and step up in their faith. Whenever you read the Bible you rarely see Jesus waiting for people to come to him. Jesus was on the move going from town-to-town, market-to-market, and temple-to-temple to meet people and love them right where they lived. His steps were calculated around his faith.

The focus of this book is *NOT* to read it only. It is to read it, think about it, pray about it, and then do something about it. The steps of faith, the steps of love, the steps of JESUSing others are more than words in this book. They are times in our lives that God has touched specifically for us. They become blessings to count. The first steps are always the toughest ones. It gets easier when we do a little more day by day. It is up to us to choose to take the first step. It is also up to us to actually take it.

*JESUSing moment>>> I know we are a little over halfway through our time together. Pray over the words you just read. Then pray about the first step you will take today in faith. Then come back tomorrow and repeat! Remember, though, the first step to JESUS others is yours!*

www.PocketFullOfFaith.com

*Just JESUS Them*

# Day 72
*Being prepared.*

---

Your JESUSing Moment                                         Date

**Ephesians 6:10–11 (NLT) *A final word: Be strong in the Lord and in his mighty power. Put on all of God's armor so that you will be able to stand firm against all strategies of the devil.***

In times of peace prepare for war. I remember reading this and thinking how much sense that made. When the war starts, if you have not trained and are not prepared, it could be over shortly. Preparation is needed physically, emotionally, and spiritually.

I once had a student in my ministry named Dara. She would always say these words to me: "JohnStahl, you rock!" (For some reason kids in my ministry always had to use my full name when addressing me. Everywhere I went I heard "JohnStahl!") Dara decided her senior year she did not want to take an English class in high school. The teacher of the class begged her to take the class. He knew the kids he had in this class and he knew that Dara could help keep the peace. He also knew she was a wonderful learner and that she would make the class exciting for the other students. Dara told the teacher she would take the class under one condition: that her youth pastor would come in and teach a lesson about something Biblical for one week. He did not hesitate for a second and made the deal.

There was one problem. Dara's youth pastor, "JohnStahl," had never taught in a class setting for one period, let alone a full week. Dara looked at me as if it was no problem and reminded me "JohnStahl, you rock!"

The high school I taught at was an intercity school. It was highly diversified in race and religious beliefs, including no beliefs at all. I taught them about Joseph from the Old Testament in the book of Genesis. Joseph was a teenager who had gone through many struggles. Joseph's struggles included sibling rivalry, being separated from his family, being charged for a crime he never committed,

*Just JESUS Them*

being looked down upon because of the color of his skin, and going to prison. All of these were struggles the students could relate to through their family, friends, and/or personally. The impact of the week could be seen on these students. Classmates started showing up to youth group. There was not a week that went by that new friends showed up with Dara for the Sunday messages at church. I was invited to come in every month to have lunch with the students in the cafeteria. They even invited me to be the speaker for their baccalaureate.

Many would tell you that the Bible has that kind of impact on people's lives. They would be correct. The messages taught from the Bible that week, the discussions around the lunch tables each month, and the message heard at the baccalaureate, would have never taken place had it not been for one student who had prepared for these battles in times of peace. Being a part of this, witnessing the student's lives changed, and watching God move in mighty ways was the blessing I got to *live*. To this day, when I see this student, I greet her with "DaraJarvis, you rock!" because she JESUSed her classmates.

**JESUSing moment>>> Be prepared. There is a battle waging around all of us. It is an eternal one. Ready yourself now before you head in to war on this day!**

www.PocketFullOfFaith.com

*Just JESUS Them*

# Day 73
*Loving your neighbor.*

---

Your JESUSing Moment Date

**Matthew 19:19 (NIV)** *"Love your neighbor as yourself."*

Bryan and Mindy live to the left of me. Carol, a widow, lives across the street from me. 'Dan the Repo Man' lives behind me. To the right of me live Jim and Barbie. They brought up four boys all starting with the letter 'A': Aaron, Andrew, Adam, and Alex.

It is amazing how time flies. You see this when you look at the ages of children. When we moved in, Bryan was next door with his mom, dad and sister. His parents moved and now Bryan is raising his family in the same house. Alex, the youngest son of Jim and Barbie, was eight years old. I used to hit him ground balls every day in my driveway when he got home from school. As he got older and my sons grew, they would line up so I could hit all of them grounders.

Carol's story is a very sad one. She and her husband Bob looked forward to retirement. Two-and-a-half months after retirement, Bob found a spot on his skin. He went in to have it examined. The diagnosis was skin cancer. It did not seem like a big deal. He went to the doctor who sent him to the hospital to have the spot surgically removed. Afterward, he was sent to a rehabilitation hospital. While going through his daily rehab routine, his health took a sudden turn for the worse. Shortly after he passed away. Everyone was in shock.

'Dan the Repo Man' is newer to the neighborhood. He and his wife just had a baby. The older children, Conner and Jessica, play with my two youngest children, Nathan and Rebecca. Our yard is the community hang out. We are happy about that. It's gives us the opportunity to get to know the kids in our neighborhood. It also gives us the opportunity to show them some love that they may not normally receive.

*Just JESUS Them*

Even more recently, across the road on the left side is a newer couple that moved in recently. I have met them once or twice. I wave to them every time I see them and say hello. For some reason, I cannot remember their names. The only name in the family I can remember is their dog's name. His name is Hank.

In this passage when Jesus said 'love your neighbor as yourself,' most of us think of the people that live around us. Jesus meant so much more than that. Your neighborhood, though, is a great place to start JESUSing others.

I shared with you today about the people who are my immediate neighbors and their names. It is not meant to brag or boast that I am any better than you. You may know more of your neighbors than I know mine! For me, I had to make an intentional choice to get to know each of them. I did so with the belief that God brought them into my life for a reason.

Today for my JESUSing moment I am going to find out the names of the owner of Hank (for the second time).

***JESUSing moment>>>** Go and love a neighbor as you would yourself. Spend some time in conversation or do something that would make their life easier, like taking out their trash, or helping with a project they want to accomplish!*

*www.PocketFullOfFaith.com*

*Just JESUS Them*

# Day 74
*Explaining salvation.*

---

Your JESUSing Moment  Date

***John 10:28 (ESV) I give them eternal life, and they will never perish, and no one will snatch them out of my hand.***

"This is the best day ever!" my son Jake exclaimed as he walked up the stairs into our dining room. He had been hanging out with two friends nearly the whole summer. This extended into the school year. The closer they grew, the stronger Jake felt about asking them to youth group. At first they declined. They always had excuses such as having other things to do, work, or just choosing not to go.

Eventually, though, they relented. They started to attend. When they attended, they heard messages about God and his love for each of them. More and more of Jake's friends joined the youth group. Many other students took notice of this personal, simple message. Two of those who noticed were Jake's two friends that he had grown close to over the past year. What was happening in this small group of friends from this high school in the middle of nowhere?

They were searching for God, and he was showing up in a powerful way. God was showing up in a personal way. God was showing up in a passionate way.

After asking question after question these two young men came to a place where they were ready to make a decision. They understood that Jesus was the only way to spend eternity in paradise. This frightens and scares many people. For me, I have found it refreshing and guilt free. The reason for this is that had God given me 1,000 choices and told me to pick one hoping it was the right way to heaven, I am sure I would choose the wrong way over and over. In his Word God showed and shared with us exactly why he sent his son Jesus. It was because he was powerful, personal, and passionate. He loved us beyond all words and recognition. And he gave for each of us that one door to choose that leads us to heaven. It took all the guesswork, the question of whether we were good

*Just JESUS Them*

enough, or hoping that we got it right on this Earth enough that God could not help but allow us into heaven. It was his gift. It was our choice to unwrap it and accept it or not.

Back to Jake's friends and this wonderful day. That evening in youth group, his two friends had accepted Christ as their personal savior. Jake was so excited for them. After they had prayed together Jake shared with them his analogy on the whole subject. What he shared with them was simple, yet powerful (don't worry, I will share that analogy with you tomorrow.)

But Jake chose to love his friends, first. Jake showed them a Jesus who loved them more than he ever could. Then he shared what you and I could share if we chose to.

**JESUSing moment>>> we all have friends we wish would grow closer to God. Rather than beat them over the head with your Bible, try showing them love in areas they may not normally receive. This is exactly what Jesus did to the people he met and loved every day!**

*www.PocketFullOfFaith.com*

## Day 75
*Explaining salvation.*

---

Your JESUSing Moment                                        Date

**John 10:28 (ESV) *I give them eternal life, and they will never perish, and no one will snatch them out of my hand.***

Yesterday I told you I would share the analogy Jake shared with his friends about salvation. Some of you may have already read ahead. If you did, the hope is you experienced a JESUSing moment or two in between the readings. (I am with you, though, as sometimes I just have to know. It's okay. Just do not forget to do the Jesus moments for each day!)

Back to today. What was that analogy that Jake shared with his two friends? Here it is. (Quick, grab someone close to you and take him/her/them through this as you read the 'instructions'!)

First, take one of your hands and hold it with your palm facing the sky. You don't need to lift your arm in the air. Have it dangle as it normally would. Now, take your other hand and point the first finger away from that palm. Allow this arm to dangle as it normally would, as well.

When someone does not know God, they are the hand that is pointing away from the hand with the palm side up. The hand with the palm side up represents God's hand. The other hand that is pointing away is you or I away from God. The reason we are pointing the other way is because we are going in the wrong direction, away from God.

Now take the hand that is pointing away and put that finger into your open palm. Close the open hand as if you were taking something off the end of the other finger and then pull the finger away. This represents you coming to God and him wrapping his loving arm around you and holding you tight.

Now take that same finger that was pointing away from the open palm hand and start poking at the newly clenched fist. Very soon

*Just JESUS Them*

you will realize you cannot open the fist. Soon after this you get tired of poking so this hand will go away and look for something else to do. Remember, in the palm of the closed hand is you being held close by God. Now take that hand that is clenched and put it up next your heart. God holds you tightly in His hand and He puts you close to His heart. Because of this, you do not have to worry about dying. Because of this, you do not have to worry about where you will be when you die. Nothing, let me repeat, NOTHING can take you out of the palm of His hand.

Jake shared this with his two friends. Light bulbs went off, smiles crossed their faces, and they understood just how much God loves them and that nothing is strong enough to separate them from that love. This is a very simple analogy. It is very powerful, as well. It came from the mind and the heart of a teenager who took the time to JESUS his friends.

*JESUSing moment>>> what led to the best day ever for Jake? Love. Do not keep this analogy to yourself. Be ready to show and share this with someone you may know who needs the same love we all need, in the palm of the hand and in the heart of God!*

www.PocketFullOfFaith.com

*Just JESUS Them*

# Day 76
*Sharing heaven.*

---

Your JESUSing Moment Date

**Luke 23:43 (ESV) And he said to him, "Truly, I say to you, today you will be with me in Paradise."**

One morning I was making breakfast sandwiches for my family. I had already made my son Nathan and my daughter Rebecca two each and decided to make one for myself. As I was getting close to finishing the sandwich, I heard a knock at our door. Nathan answered it. I heard a brief conversation, heard him say thank you, and heard the door shut. He walked into the kitchen and handed me a pamphlet. It was a Jehovah's Witness pamphlet. He told me they told us to go to a website to find out more information about them. I found it interesting that they were using the Internet to reach others. I have heard countless people say very negative things about Jehovah's Witnesses. I give them credit, as they are not afraid to go out to try and reach others for what they feel is the cause for Christ. Sadly, they are being misled. Remember, though, that if they are brave enough to walk into a strange neighborhood to reach others, we can brave enough to love them back and try to help them get on the right path leading to God.

After Nathan handed me the pamphlet, I finished making my sandwich. I made sure the stove was off and, with sandwich in hand (it was a really good sandwich and you can't leave food lying around my kids or it will be gone when you come back for it), I ran outside to call out to the girls that came to the door. I showed off my shyness immediately as I yelled out "HEY!" in a loud voice. The women were walking down my neighbor's driveway two doors down. They just stared at me. I yelled "HEY!" again and waved. Once again they just stared and kept walking. Just then I heard a quiet voice say, "Excuse me, sir?" I looked down my driveway and there were the two women who dropped off the pamphlet at my door. I was yelling at the wrong women. This is part of my charm.

*Just JESUS Them*

Undaunted, and with my sandwich in hand, I asked them to come and talk with me.

The next 15 minutes were filled with a discussion about faith. I was saddened to see how misdirected they were. The further we dove into Scripture the more I shared God's love for them. I told them over and over I did not want to judge them and I did not want them to feel any guilt. I did want to show them that God loves them just as they are and has a place waiting for them in heaven just as he does me. I shared with them that I felt it was great that they were willing to share their faith that day. I also wanted them to know that they could be certain that they had a place in eternity with Jesus in heaven, and showed them this in the Bible they carried. I let them know that if they ever wanted to come back to talk more to feel free to do so. I would even make them a sandwich.

Part of me felt as though I had failed. Eventually, though, I realized I did all I could to Jesus them that day.

*JESUSing moment>>>How do you react when someone knocks on the door or rings the doorbell? What if we treated these moments as if God was knocking on the door, and sending us a visitor? Ready yourself for times such as these. It may not be a physical knocking on your door, but someone will come into your path soon that you will have the opportunity to show Jesus to him or her.*

*www.PocketFullOfFaith.com*

## Day 77

*I write to those who belong to Christ Jesus and to those who are set apart by Him and made holy. I write to all the Christians everywhere who call on the name of Jesus Christ.* **That is from Paul in 1 Corinthians 1:2 (NLV). It is a reminder and encouragement as to why we write and journal!**

*Just JESUS Them*

www.PocketFullOfFaith.com

*Just JESUS Them*

# Day 78
*Adopting a child.*

---

Your JESUSing Moment  Date

***John 14:18 (ESV) I will not leave you as orphans; I will come to you.***

(Before I start let me share with you that I am not expecting you to go out and actually adopt a child. I understand this can be very expensive. At the same time, maybe God is leading you in that direction. I don't want to discount that, either.)

On a trip taken to a foreign country many years ago, one of our daily visits was to an orphanage. I cannot say the name of the country due to there being so few orphanages there. I don't want to take a chance that this could affect these children in any way. While visiting this orphanage we found that many of the children there actually had parents that were still alive. Because they did not have a lot of money they dropped the children off at the orphanage knowing that they would be fed daily and have a roof over their head to sleep under each and every night. The parents would come to visit their children, but the kids would call them their aunt or uncle. The interesting thing was most of the workers at the orphanage knew this was taking place. They also knew the families struggled financially and that this was the only way to raise the child and fulfill their needs.

Once we found this was taking place, we looked at the visitors in a different light. They were allowed to spend two hours a day with their child. While that might sound heart breaking, it was also time that was devoted strictly by the parents to their children.

Living in the United States, we are blessed with so many freedoms. We tend to take those for granted. One of those freedoms is the time that we are able to spend with our children. Sadly, many parents spend little to no time with their kids on a daily basis. Parents are so busy running their children from event to event, from a practice to a field, from a court to a school, that they spend very little quality time together. Even though we have all the freedoms this country has to offer, we miss out on this quality time with our children. It is as if our children are orphans growing up in their own home. Yet statistic after statistic, research paper after research paper, and study after study proves that the most well adjusted children are the ones who have time every day with mom and dad or guardian. Those same studies prove that our children crave this time with their parents. You read that correctly. Our kids actually want to be with us as parents or someone that is an adult they can talk with, spend quality time with, and trust.

Today, why not adopt a child? When I say this, I mean spend some quality time with a child in your life. It could be a neighborhood kid, a niece or nephew, a cousin, and especially your own child or children. As the verse of the day says: let us not leave them as orphans. Let us take the first step and go to him or her and Jesus them instead!

***JESUSing moment>>> Remember that Jesus loved the children. Make the most of this time and make sure that what you do is honoring to God. If it is your biological child, you have been blessed. Make the most of this time with that blessing today!***

www.PocketFullOfFaith.com

*Just JESUS Them*

## Day 79
*Timing is everything.*

**Your JESUSing Moment**                                                   Date

**Ecclesiastes 3:1-2b (NLV) [A Time for Everything] There is a special time for everything. There is a time for everything that happens under heaven. There is a time to be born, and a time to die.**

I have a friend who died too young. He was 18 when he was involved in a car accident. He was in the passenger side of the car. The driver did not see the stop sign in time and tried to make the best of the situation. Unfortunately, he went through the stop sign as he tried to turn left at the same time. He hit a van driving at a high rate of speed. The van hit the side of the car with my friend in the passenger seat.

The driver of the car has never been the same. Nor have the three kids that were sitting in the backseat. One of them was ejected from the rear window of the car. The only one that lost their life in the accident was my friend that was in the passenger seat, Robbie. A couple of the people in the car were in my graduating class from high school. The other ones were a year younger. They live every day rehashing this accident in their hearts and their minds.

It was a grim and sad reminder of how quickly life can change. It can happen in an instance. In fact, it can happen as quickly as snapping your fingers.

Most of us have had a reminder such as this in our lifetime. It could have been a friend or family member who was at fault in an accident. It could have been a friend or family member who was the victim in the accident. It could have been a friend or family member who lost his or her life. Regardless of who was at fault, those that are lost are examples of people we love.

An accident such as this was a wake up call to the importance to care for and love others every day. None of us know when the time may end for ourselves or our friends and family. Like Robbie, like you, like me, and like every person we come in contact with daily, there will be a time for this. The one thing that is certain in this life is that none of us will make it out physically alive.

Jesus promises eternity to those who trust and believe in Him. That is why we Jesus others. It is also why Jesus JESUS'ed others and still JESUS's each one of us every day.

*JESUSing moment>>> if there truly is a time for everything as the Bible teaches, does that mean there is a time for us to be resolved with our maker? We can know for sure we have a place with him in heaven. It is to all that trust and believe. If you have not taken that step and asked God to save you, maybe the best way to JESUS someone today is to JESUS your self and ask him to be your counselor, your guide, and your savior. It is all part of God's perfect timing.*

www.PocketFullOfFaith.com

*Just JESUS Them*

# Day 80

*Living with resolve.*

| Your JESUSing Moment | Date |
|---|---|

**1 Timothy 4:8b (NIV) Godliness has value for all things, holding promise for both the present life and the life to come.**

I have heard many people say, "I should write a book!", myself included. It could be about life lessons such as being a parent. It could be from experiences learned such as a teacher from her classroom. Or, it could be about something that nobody else knows much about, but have always wanted to learn, and you are just the person to teach them.

When I became the lead pastor at the church I am currently serving, a young man came into my office with that same desire of writing a book, and asked if I would read it. He had just started writing and wanted an opinion about the content and how it read. I told him to bring it in when he was finished and I would take a look at it for him.

A few months went by with me seeing this young man sparingly. That changed as I started seeing him each and every Sunday until one day he showed up carrying something in a bag. Before service started he asked if he could talk to me in my office when we were finished with the first service. I told him that was not a problem.

We walked into my office between services when he pulled the item he was carrying from the bag. It was his book. And when I say it was a book, I am not talking about a pamphlet or a quick read. The monstrosity that he set before me was hundreds of pages long and included character breakdowns, storylines, and pictures. He had already talked to a publisher, as he was getting ready for it to go to production. He wanted me to have a copy and asked me to continue to pray that this would reach others.

To put it bluntly, I was amazed. I asked him how much time this took him to do the project. He told me he worked every day at his regular job but when he got home he started writing. Some days only a few words would come. Other days, thousands upon thousands of words poured out of his heart and mind onto the pages. When it was finished the final copy had over 135,000 words in it. I sat stunned and shocked. I was in awe of the work that he had produced. I was even more in awe of the resolve he had to finish the project.

Do you realize that every day we are a work of the Lord? He molds us and shapes us and prepares us to love and reach others in his name. He wants us to share the good news of eternity and how simple it is to know for sure that you have a place with him when you leave this earth. When he puts something on our heart, however, it is up to you and me to be resolved enough to see the project through for the One who put the project on our heart.

I am so resolved about this issue that I have considered writing a book about it. Wait . . .

***JESUSing moment>>> what is that one thing you have always wanted to do for God? Take today to start back on the project, or to start a new one. Be resolved to finish the project as part of your every day love for others!***

*www.PocketFullOfFaith.com*

*Just JESUS Them*

# Day 81
*Looking with our heart.*

---

Your JESUSing Moment                              Date

**1 Samuel 16:7 (NLV) But the Lord said to Samuel, "Do not look at the way he looks on the outside or how tall he is, because I have not chosen him. For the Lord does not look at the things man looks at. A man looks at the outside of a person, but the Lord looks at the heart."**

A friend of mine recently started attending church. This is a huge step for him because as a young child his home church turned on him and his family. He was sure he would never set foot in a church again. Over time his heart softened. Surrounding himself with the right people, he found himself attending church once again. In fact, he and his family attended every week. He had made it a New Year's resolution and he stuck with it.

Like every great story there has to be a plot twist. This story is no different. And the twist was this: he loved to wear baseball cap. All the time, everywhere, regardless of the day or time of day, you would find him wearing a baseball cap. This included to church.

For some reason, another friend of mine did not like the fact that this man wore a baseball cap in church. It was something he had grown up with and been taught. A person took their hat off for the National Anthem, when you entered a building, and especially in church. Each week my friend with his resolution would show up to church and sit and listen to the message in his baseball cap. Each week, my other friend would see him and try to figure out a way to say something to him so he would stop wearing the hat in church.

Thankfully, the second gentleman came to me first before saying something to the man in the hat. At first, our discussion centered on the fact that he was going to talk to the gentleman in the hat no matter what. He knew his stance and he was not going to change this stance. It was how he was brought up and he was going to stick with it no matter what. I started sharing verses with him from the Bible. The first one I shared is the verse for today. Slowly but surely, he started to soften his stance. In the process he shared with me that he was studying his Bible at a deeper level.

In the end, he softened his stance to the point that he was not going to say a word to the gentleman in the hat, other than being kind and greeting him. In fact, he totally understood that it was more important to focus on the heart of the man than the hat a man might wear on his head.

For many of us we have had times like this that we struggle to face. We were taught things by parents or other loved ones and it is difficult to let it go. Be careful not to let your past mess with your present to the point it could stop you in your walk for the future.

**JESUSing moment>>> what is it that is difficult to let go? Whatever that one thing might be, is it getting in the way of you caring for others? We need to learn to put that in the past so we can care for others today and in the future.**

*www.PocketFullOfFaith.com*

*Just JESUS Them*

# Day 82

*Living your dash.*

---

**Your JESUSing Moment**            Date

**James 4:14 (TLB) *How do you know what is going to happen tomorrow? For the length of your lives is as uncertain as the morning fog—now you see it; soon it is gone.***

We all have that one person in our life that has said something to us that somehow stuck. Maybe it was a coworker, a teacher/professor, or a friend, but they said something in such a way that you can not help at times in your life hearing his or her voice and their words. A life event brought that voice to your mind. What they said suddenly brought more meaning than you ever realized until that moment and their words collided.

My first pastor, friend, and mentor, Dallas Billington, once asked this question during his message. "How are you living your dash?" For me, the question stuck in both my mind and my heart.

I had never been asked that question and I was not quite sure what he meant. Dallas explained further that every one of us had a date we were born. Each of us has a date we will die. The interesting point for all of us was the part in between these two dates that lasted the longest. That was our 'dash.' Yet for most of us, life has not been a dash. It has been a marathon.

How have we filled that dash? Is it filled up with entertainment such as TV, movies, or video games? Maybe we have found our self at happy hour every day or out partying with friends on the weekends. Some of us have done things in private we thought we would have never done yet they have continued to this day. Others have wasted away in isolation. Others, still, have washed their hands of people and do all they can to distance themselves with long hikes, rides, or travels. Regardless, if any of these are things you have done, are doing, or have planned to do to get away, it begs the question: "How are you living your dash?"

*Just JESUS Them*

I have thought about that message from Dallas many, many times. For some reason it stuck. The verse he used that day was from James (at the beginning of our day). To this day

I have asked myself the question many, many times. You would have thought by now I would have stopped. I have not, because my dash and how I have lived it has continued.

Today, however, I JESUS you and have extended that same question to you. Pause for a moment and reflect and ask yourself: "How am I living my dash?"

***JESUSing moment>>> How are you living your dash? Who have you been living your dash for each day? Time to make a dash and live part of your dash by JESUSing someone today and every day!***

www.PocketFullOfFaith.com

*Just JESUS Them*

## Day 83
*Killing sacred cows.*

---

Your JESUSing Moment                                                 Date

**Leviticus 26:1 (NLV) Do not make gods for yourselves. Do not set up for yourselves something to look like a god or a holy object. Do not set up something cut from stone in your land to bow down to. For I am the Lord your God.**

I lead and attend a church that is 113 years old. Finding anything this age that is still active and alive is rare. Whether it is a person, a company, or a church, things today just do not seem to last like they used to. The older things get, however, the more difficult it is to change. We get used to it being a certain way and we expect it to stay like that. In the church, this could mean many things. It could be the style of music. It could mean reading from a certain Bible version. It could mean only having songs performed from the hymnals. It could even mean having parts of the service that you are used to and not willing to let go.

I have a family that I consider good friends. They left their old church to attend ours because of a song that was no longer sung at Christmas. The funny thing is, I cannot imagine people *not* singing this song at Christmas. Yet, for whatever reason, this church decided to stop singing 'Silent Night.' For me, that is a song we will always sing at Christmas, at least as long as I am leading the church. Could this change? Absolutely. Just not on my watch.

I never want to be someone who gets stuck in my ways. This got me thinking about whether I am becoming a stodgy old person or if I am willing to change? I believe I am still willing to change, if it makes sense for the whole of the church body. What I have found with people in the church, however, are there are certain parts they cannot let go. These are often referred to as sacred cows. As long as the sacred cows are alive, people are happy. If you mess with a sacred cow, be ready for a fight.

Recently, I talked about sacrificing one of these sacred cows. The response I received back from a few people shocked me. I could not believe how quickly voices rose. I could not believe the range of emotions and how quickly they escalated. I realized how sacred a cow could be. It was to the point where people would leave the church or would rally people to force leaders from their positions in the church just to keep their sacred cow. In the end, the sacred cow was more important than a close friendship.

Whether we realize it or not, we all have sacred cows. These are areas in our lives that we have put ahead of God. To be quite frank, these cows need to be sacrificed if they are getting in the way of us showing Jesus to someone else.

*JESUSing moment>>> what is your sacred cow? What is getting in the way of you spending time to love others? Is it a bad habit, a material possession, or something you just cannot let go of that you have held onto for years? Whatever it might be, are you willing to put that sacred cow aside to show someone some love? Think about it. Is that the same thing God did for us when he sacrificed His son?*

www.PocketFullOfFaith.com

## Day 84

Paul wrote in 2 Corinthians 2:4 (NLT): I wrote that letter in great anguish . . . to let you know how much I loved you. What moments can you write about to remind yourself of the moment you loved others this week?

*Just JESUS Them*

www.PocketFullOfFaith.com

*Just JESUS Them*

## Day 85
*Making it last.*

---

Your JESUSing Moment                                    Date

**Joshua 10:13a (NLT) So the sun stood still and the moon stayed in place.**

We all have moments in our life that seem to last an eternity. We could be waiting for a letter in the mail. When it finally shows up, the time of whether or not to open it can be excruciating. Time does not 'fly by' in that moment. It goes by frame by frame. If you have ever been in a car accident you can go back and relive each step as if every instant was an event in and of itself. For some people walking down the aisle could be that moment, for many reasons. It could be for the dad that is about to give his little girl away, a mom who is waiting up front for her daughter, the groom who is yet to see his soon-to-be wife for the first time that day, or the bride who is walking next to her father as a single woman one last time. For those of us who have children; holding your newborn child qualifies as one of those moments. Time stood still and you remember it as if they were yesterday.

The birth of our second child was one of those moments for me, personally. Jacob was a January 1st due date child. It was amazing how many people shared with me that we needed to have him before January 1st. The reason for this is we would get a tax break. The funny thing is, they were serious. I kept praying for a happy, healthy child. Not once did I ever think to pray for a tax break baby. I obviously needed to get my priorities straight.

Sadly, at least for my taxes that year, Jacob decided to come out three days later on January 4th. Before I had that moment where I could hold him the first time there was that moment that lasted for what seemed like an eternity. The doctor held Jacob up, he was purple, and he was not breathing. I felt a huge lump in my throat. At that moment, I could not breathe myself as time stood still.

*Just JESUS Them*

The doctor started talking to Jacob. "Come on little buddy don't make me come in there." He was shaking Jacob ever so slightly. Jacob was not responding. I looked at the doctor and then back to Jacob. He still was not breathing. The doctor was very calm. Just as he was about to lay Jacob down to work on him further something kick-started for Jacob. He took his first breath. Then another. Then another. Our three-day late child was starting to breathe on his own. Normal color was appearing in his face and body. For our Jacob, his clock was officially starting to tick. For everyone else in the room, the clock began ticking again. When you finally reach that moment you cannot help but take a huge breath yourself.

We all have moments that make the clock stop. They could be huge life-changing events. They could be something that stops us in our tracks just long enough to get our attention. Either way, these are moments to reflect on what God is doing in our lives. You may not have that 'stop in your tracks moment' today. "Your JESUSing Moment" and "Date." But all of us will have that moment sooner or later. Be ready for the moment that time is standing still.

**JESUSing moment>>> Be prepared to spend time with someone close to you may have a moment like this. It may sound simple, but it could mean more to the person on the other end than any of us even realize in that moment.**

www.PocketFullOfFaith.com

*Just JESUS Them*

# Day 86 (Part 1)
*Making a visit.*

---

Your JESUSing Moment                                        Date

**Acts 15:36 (NLV) "Let us go back and visit the Christians in every city where we have preached the Word of God. Let us see how they are doing."**

Everyone has a favorite time of the year. I live in Ohio so for me, personally, it is the fall. The running joke in Ohio is that if you want the weather to change all you have to do is wait for the next day. One particular week started off with one of the hottest days on record. It rained the next full day, as we caught the back end of a hurricane. The following day it was sunny, yet cloudy, but crisp and beautiful and you could enjoy the leaves changing colors in the trees. By the weekend we had both sleet and snow. Such is life and the weather in Ohio.

When the weather is nice I love to get outside and enjoy the day. When it is raining, sleeting, or snowing, I would rather chill out and relax. Fall is the best time when it comes to sports, as well. Major League Baseball has its playoffs, college and pro football are both in full swing, and both basketball and hockey are just getting underway with their seasons.

One Sunday I was enjoying a football game on TV. It was Sunday afternoon and I was as comfortable as I could be. It just so happened on this day people were making a visit from the church in my neighborhood. I was the leader of this group whenever the actual leader was not available. This was one of those days. I was not happy with the situation. Thankfully, the time came and passed when the people were supposed to meet at my house to go and visit the person in my neighborhood. Almost 30 minutes had passed and I realized I was home free and could sit and enjoy the football game. At that moment, a car pulled into my driveway. The game was on a commercial break, so I opened the door and invited them into my house. I explained to them how instead of going into the neighborhood to make a visit, I would train them on some important things that no one else had taught them, such as how to truly 'reach' people. None of them seemed to like the idea. Realizing we were going to have to go and visit my neighbor, I reluctantly put on my shoes and jacket to head out the door.

My neighbor was gone most of the time, so I hoped he would be anywhere but his house as we approached his door. I knocked on the door. There was no answer. I turned to leave when one of the people in the group asked if I would try again. I did so, and still there was no answer. I started to head back down the steps when the other gentleman in the group knocked on the door even louder. I stared at him and took my place back at the front of the group directly in front of my neighbor's door. I knew there was no way he was home and that football was calling me. At the same time, I needed to appease the group. As we were all ready to give up, the door opened a couple inches. There was darkness inside but I heard a voice say my name. "John?" The door swung open and there stood a man in tears. What came next I will share over the next couple days. Had I not taken this step, and had the people with me not pushed me, I am not sure I would be the same to this day.

***JESUSing moment>>> who came to mind or to your heart when you read this devotional today? Who ever that might be, stop by and see them today.***

www.PocketFullOfFaith.com

*Just JESUS Them*

# Day 87 (Part 2)
*Battling life.*

---

Your JESUSing Moment                                    Date

***John 16:33 (NLT) I have told you all this so that you may have peace in me. Here on earth you will have many trials and sorrows. But take heart, because I have overcome the world."***

Standing face-to-face with a man in tears was not a position any of us would desire. Yet, there I stood with three people I barely knew facing my neighbor who looked both scared and bewildered. I gave him the standard church visitation line, as I had nothing else to say. "Do you mind if we come in and sit down and talk for little while?" I asked. We followed John (my neighbor's name, as well) into his house to his living room. John placed the items in his hand onto his cluttered coffee table. The couches had newspapers and old mail stacked everywhere. There was literally nowhere to sit. After frantically clearing off the couches, we all had a seat and sat down for a visit.

At first the conversation was light-hearted. I talked to John about the things we normally discussed, such as how the Cleveland Indians (our local and favorite team) had played this season. John finally gathered himself enough to where I felt we could have a normal conversation. He had recently visited our church and filled out a communication card that he found in the pew. He checked the little box asking for a visit and prayer. It was then that I found out something that blew me away. John was not a first time visitor to the church. In fact, he attended the same church that I did, and both he and his wife had done so for over a decade. Yet, over the years we had never seen one another. Not one time. Granted, the church we attended was a very large church. It is what many would describe today as a mega church as over 2000 people where in attendance on any given Sunday. John shared with me how he not only attended the church, but he had worked in children's ministry for years. In fact, he worked in one department while his wife worked in another ministry elsewhere in the church.

*Just JESUS Them*

This led me to my next question, which was this: why did he fill out the communication card that was there for the visitors? He shared with me that every Sunday he had been in his department with the children. He had never seen these cards because he was never in the main service. That was his first time in many years to attend and listen to a message from our pastor. So, for him, it was as if he was visiting for the first time. John needed another adult to talk to as all of his attention had been on the children at the church. To put it bluntly, he needed help and he needed someone to talk to right away.

John stared blankly into my eyes. You could see that he was in a fog. His next sentences went right to the heart of his struggles. "I work hard to take care of my family. I put in extra hours to take care of their every need. I watched as my oldest two boys grew up and graduated, and my little girl independent. And now my wife is leaving me for another man."

His words hit us all like a ton of bricks. It was our turn to stare blankly back at John.

***JESUSing moment>>> we all have moments to stop us in our tracks. It is called life. Who is it in your life that needs your ear and your attention TODAY?***

www.PockctFullOfFaith.com

Just JESUS Them

# Day 88 (Part 3)
*Sharing good news.*

---

Your JESUSing Moment                              Date

**Matthew 7:7b (NLT) "Keep on seeking, and you will find."**

John shared more with us that day. John was a hard worker who had put in a ton of overtime at work because he wanted to take his family on a nice vacation. He did not attend any of his kid's extra curricular events because of work. For some reason, in his mind, a nice vacation would help bring them all back together. He worked odd hours so that while he was sleeping his kids were at school and while he was working his kids were home. His wife worked the opposite schedule to be there for the kids when they got home from school. He thought that was part of the plan.

The schedule took its toll on his family. John stopped going to church other than to serve in the children's ministry when it was his month. He could not remember the last time he had heard a message in the main service. All he and his wife were doing was serving the children of the church on Sunday morning. After church, they came home and John slept so he could work again that night. Every meaningful relationship he had in his life had deteriorated. His relationship with God was distant. His relationship with his wife was nearly nonexistent. As a dad, he hardly even knew his kids. He did not know their interests, how they were doing in school, or who any of their friends were. He was worse than a distant dad. He had become invisible.

The question he kept asking himself over and over that day was "Why?" Why did he have to work so much? Why did he stop attending church services? Why did he stop spending time with his family? Why did he become so distant from his wife?

With any visit from our church, you are taught first to listen. The more he shared with us the more my heart went out to him. Eventually, we asked him some questions, and asked if was resolved in his relationship with God? Had he ever taken the time

*Just JESUS Them*

to accept the gift that God offered to each of us through his son, Jesus? Did he trust and believe that God had sent his Son to die on the cross for him and that we would have a place in heaven?

John looked directly into my eyes. For all the years that he had gone to church, he had heard about Jesus, was taught about Jesus, yet he had never taken the time to ask Him into his heart. On our visit that day, John took the time. By the end of our conversation, he was resolved that he had a place in heaven with Jesus. As we finished praying together it was my turn to look John in the eyes. They were filled with tears as he could barely keep his emotions. I went over and sat next to him. I put my hand on the back of his neck as he sobbed uncontrollably. It was then that I noticed the things that he had carried in his hand earlier and put on the table in front of him.

It was yet another opportunity to be shocked that day. It was also a reminder of the importance of JESUSing others every day.

***JESUSing moment>>> if you are a believer you know what it means to be resolved with God. You know the greatest story ever and are a part of that story personally. When was the last time you shared that personal moment with someone?***

www.PocketFullOfFaith.com

*Just JESUS Them*

# Day 89 (Part 4)
*Knocking on a door.*

---

**Your JESUSing Moment**                                        Date

**Matthew 7:7a,c (NLT) "Keep on asking, and you will receive what you ask for . . . Keep on knocking, and the door will be opened to you.**

Sitting in front of John on the coffee table were the items he had in his hand when he answered the door that day. I had not noticed the items at the time he placed them there. The reason for this was all the clutter everywhere else in the room. John was clearing places for us to sit down and we were distracted from what was in his hand. Yet there were the items on the tables and suddenly they were staring at us as if they were the only other things in the room.

On the table in front of us sat his car keys, a small hose, and a roll of duct tape. I looked into John's eyes and asked him what these were for and why he was carrying them.

John squirmed a little bit in his seat. He did not want to make eye contact. Remember, I was the only person he truly knew on a personal level in the room. The other people that were with me he was meeting for the first time. But there was nowhere else for him to go.

John finally came up with the nerve, and was able to compose himself enough to speak. Looking at me with tears in his eyes, he shared with me why he had these items and what he intended to do with them. "The reason it took me so long to answer the front door today was because I was heading out the back door. I was at the end of my rope and I could see no other way out. I just wanted it to end. I was hoping that God would give me a way out. I stood at the back door for the longest time with my car keys, the hose, and the duct tape in my hands. I could not find the strength to turn the doorknob to head out to the garage to get in my car. I was finally at that point and I grabbed the doorknob when I heard a knock at the front door. I wanted to ignore it, but you kept knocking. I

*Just JESUS Them*

decided to at least look to see who it was that was at the front door. When I saw that it was you, I knew I had to answer the door. Had I not done that, well . . ." His voice trailed off to the silence left in the room.

I knew. Even though I knew, I was shocked. Thoughts of wanting to watch a football game went through my head. Thoughts of selfishness and not caring for loving my neighbor did, too. Had the people that day not prodded me, not been persistent, and not shown up when they did, John would have been dead.

There are still days some 20 years later that I think about this day. I thank God that he brought the right people at the right time into my life. At just the right time, within these God moments, he sent ones to help give me the strength to walk across the road, knock on the door of my neighbor, and Jesus someone.

*JESUSing moment>>> we never want to look back and have regrets. We all have the person we wished we had called, reached out to, or stopped by to visit. Today is about going to knock on that someone's door. Do not put it off. Knock on their door today. It may be their home or their office, but it is time to take that step!*

www.PocketFullOfFaith.com

*Just JESUS Them*

# Day 90
*Showing tough love.*

---

Your JESUSing Moment            Date

**Matthew 23:13 (The Message) "I've had it with you! You're hopeless, you religion scholars, you Pharisees! Frauds! Your lives are roadblocks to God's kingdom. You refuse to enter, and won't let anyone else in either."**

We all have that person in our life that cannot help but get in his or her own way. It can be for a variety of reasons. He or she may have to be right all the time. He or she may only know one way, his or hers, and it is the only way. The fact is, many times they are correct. It is not what they say or do but the means by which they do these. What they do not realize is how many people they turn off or push away in the process. Many times it is as if they do not even care. As long as they are right at the end of the day, nothing else really matters.

How is it though, we can Jesus people like this in our lives? The first thing we have to remember is we have to be very careful not to enable them. We can be encouraging, but we still cannot accept this type of behavior. They will want to argue their point over and over to the point it can be exhausting. So at some point you have to tell them this is a growing process for them, but they have to quit acting like they are currently. Guess what happens every time after this discussion? You guessed it: he or she does it again. That means the process starts over on both sides. They have to be right, and you have to figure out if you want to put up with this any longer.

This is where the term 'tough love' comes into play. You have to understand that some people have no desire to change. They may even believe in God, believe in Jesus, and read their Bible. Still, at the end of the day they do what they want to do regardless of whom it affects on the other end. If you have talked to them about this, have tried to help them, yet over and over there is no desire to change, it may be time to show them that "tough love." Showing tough love means you may need to change the

*Just JESUS Them*

relationship. Showing tough love means you may need to dismiss them from a position or leadership role. Showing tough love may also mean you no longer have that person in the same position they are in relationship to *you* in your life. *(NOTE: I want to be clear that I am in no way referring to people's marriages. That is a covenant before God that you both made and you need to work through it. Seeing a Christian counselor and committing to at least one year of counseling together is a great start in getting that devotion to one another back.)*

I am sure some of you are thinking right now how is this possibly 'JESUSing' anyone? If you reread the verses from today, you will see there were times when Jesus had to show some 'tough love.' The Pharisees wanted nothing more than to be correct; to make the rules, and to make sure everyone knew how important they were. Sometimes even Jesus had to show tough love!

*JESUSing moment>>> this moment is a little bit out of the norm. It is not your normal JESUSing moment. If you have people like this in your life and you find yourself exhausted or fearful because of them, ask yourself this question: do you want to live your life as a reflection of Jesus or do you want to allow this other person to exhaust you to the point where you do not have the energy to Jesus anyone?*

www.PocketFullOfFaith.com

## Day 91

Revelation 1:19 (NLT) says "Write down what you have seen—both the things that are now happening and the things that will happen." We can do the same. Maybe you have some ideas on how to JESUS others that you have not read in the book. Make notes so you can create your own JESUSing moments, as well!

*Just JESUS Them*

www.PocketFullOfFaith.com

*Just JESUS Them*

# Day 92
*Dealing with divorce.*

---

Your JESUSing Moment                                        Date

***Matthew 19:5-6 (NLT) And JESUS said "'This explains why a man leaves his father and mother and is joined to his wife, and the two are united into one.' Since they are no longer two but one, let no one split apart what God has joined together."***

If you have never heard the saying "divorce is tougher than death on a person" I am here today to share with you how true that is. In dealing with death you have closure. There is a headstone or an urn where a body or ashes are housed. In divorce, the person who used to be your spouse is still there every day. Each time you see the person you were once married to, there are reminders of what used to be. Couple that feeling with the memories of what caused the separation in your relationship, which eventually led to divorce, and there is even more daily pain added. If a child or children are part of the equation the pain is multiplied exponentially. The age of the child or children can also add to the pain. If their ages are pre-school age or in elementary school, you have no choice but to come face to face with a former spouse for over a decade. If your children are older, such as in middle school or high school, you now have to deal with a teenager's personal issues of trust. Think of it this way: the relationship they grew to trust the most, their mom and dad, is broken, so how can they ever get to the point that they will trust another person and "live happily after"?

Everywhere you turn the decisions made that lead to divorce is anxiety and frustration that you live with for days, months, years, and, for some, what seems like a lifetime. Even worse, people that used to be *your* friends are no longer a part of *your* life because of the divorce. Where did they go? Why did they go? Will I ever have people like that in my life again? What is wrong with me? Do people know that I am divorced? Will I be shunned in public? What about at work or in school? Question after unanswerable question consume your every thought and action. You question relationships you had. You question the relationships you lost. You question yourself in these relationships. You continue to question, question, and question everything—including God.

For people that have gone through this devastating life experience, knowing that someone loves them can help in their recovery. We all know someone who is going through or has gone through divorce. It is not as if we have to call them up and discuss the divorce. We can reach out to them, love them, and show them that we care. It could help this person start down the path to heal the most important relationship for any of us: God, who is the ultimate healer. When they find healing in this relationship, God can help answer all the questions that never had answers that they still ask themselves daily.

***JESUSing moment>>> When reading this someone came to your mind. It may even be yourself. It could be a parent, the child, a friend, or coworker. Go today and show them that they can be loved. It could help take them away from the vicious cycle asking all these questions that they cannot answer. Instead, it could help them focus on a new relationship that God has brought to them today, and find those answers in His healing.***

*www.PocketFullOfFaith.com*

Just JESUS Them

## Day 93
*Making a first impression.*

---
Your JESUSing Moment                                   Date

**Luke 2:25–28 (The Voice) While fulfilling these sacred obligations at the temple, they encountered a man in Jerusalem named Simeon. He was a just and pious man, anticipating the liberation of Israel from her troubles. He was a man in touch with the Holy Spirit. The Holy Spirit had revealed to Simeon that he would not die before he had seen the Lord's Anointed One. The Spirit had led him to the temple that day, and there he saw the child Jesus in the arms of His parents, who were fulfilling their sacred obligations. Simeon took Jesus into his arms and blessed God.**

"You never get a second chance to make a first impression."

I remember hearing that when I was younger and thinking "Who cares?" If people do not like me, deal with it. Don't like how I dress? Don't look. Don't like how I talk? Don't listen. Don't like how my hair is cut, or my earring—go some place else. (Yes, I had an earring. I wore it in my left ear. When my dad saw it for the first time I thought he was going to go through the roof. When my grandma saw it for the first time she loved it. She even left me her diamond earrings when she passed away. Aren't grandmas awesome?) I am who I am, and that is how I will stay.

It is funny how time softens us and changes our perspective. Nowadays, it is not that I do not care about my first impression; I just want it to reflect more of what is going on the inside—not what is seen on the outside.

So, let me give you three terms, and think about YOUR first impression when you read each one. Before I do, all I ask is that you take a little time and truly think about the first thing that goes through your head when you read them, even if you have been introduced to them in the past:

*Just JESUS Them*

God. Holy Spirit. Jesus.

Isn't it interesting that we have been taught that these are one and the same? They are, literally 3-in-1. (If you are a math nut, the equation is simple: 1 x 1 x 1 = 1. Some think it is 1+1+1, but that would equal 3!) When you and I think of these individually, we get a different first impression. Or, at least, I do. So, what are your first impressions when you read each one?

What is it that they impress upon you? Remember, "You never get a second chance to make a first impression."

***JESUSing moment>>> Prepare yourself to make a first impression today. You will meet someone for the first time. What is the most important thing will you show or share with them for this first encounter?***

www.PocketFullOfFaith.com

*Just JESUS Them*

## Day 94
*Asking questions.*

---

Your JESUSing Moment                                                    Date

**Matthew 16:26 (TLB) What profit is there if you gain the whole world—and lose eternal life? What can be compared with the value of eternal life?**

(We played this game on Day 57, but felt the need to bring it back.) Would you rather go bald or have your hair turn gray at a very young age? Would you rather lose the ability to speak or to smell?

Before you say neither, what if you *HAD* to pick one? I have posed these (and many other) questions over time to people. I love to hear their responses. I have found that what they *LOVE* to do is at the very central point of their answers.

After asking one of these questions, listen to their entire answer. If they do not offer any reasoning after making their choice, which is rare, then ask them that all-important follow up question: "Why?" The answers you receive may or may not surprise you. They are signs to what is important to the people God has placed in your life.

For example, devout runners would rather have their legs and live with only one arm. A guitarist would keep his or her arms over a leg. Teens who play video games for hours on end would rather lose their hearing so they could still see the game as they play. A person who loves the outdoors and relaxes to its sounds would rather keep his hearing to enjoy those sounds even more every morning and evening.

Now that you know how the game is played, and hopefully answered those questions for yourself, let me ask you another question. Would you rather go to heaven and not be sure who is going to be there with you, or would you rather go to heaven and know for sure that your loved ones will be there, too?

Jesus is asking us this very question in the reading today (Matthew 16:26). It is the same question that we can ask our friends and

*Just JESUS Them*

loved ones. Remember, you (and him or her) HAVE to choose one answer. So, here it is: Would you rather have all the riches of this world, and not go to heaven, or know for sure you are going to heaven and be completely broke and poor in this life?

You may have a wonderful life and everything this world has to offer. On top of this you may know Christ as your personal savior. You have both. What about the ones you love? Do they have both? Do they have one without the other? Do they have neither?

Would you rather ask them this question or, being a believer, would you rather not ask and just hope that they have the same answer as you?

***JESUSing moment>>> Make a list today of the people you can ask this question. Listen to their response and be ready to share your thoughts and your answer as well. This may be the most important question you ever ask someone.***

*www.PocketFullOfFaith.com*

## Day 95
*Filling a God-Shaped Hole.*

---

Your JESUSing Moment                                        Date

**Psalm 23:4 (NIV) Even though I walk through the darkest valley, I will fear no evil, for you are with me; your rod and your staff, they comfort me.**

I remember the phone call as if it were yesterday. On the other end of the line was my friend Doug. He shared with me how he had not one, but two heart attacks. He could not believe he was alive. He was not the only one. Doctors and nurses told him he should have been dead. For some reason he was not. He was still here and he was wondering "Why?"

As our conversation continued there was one thing that was very obvious. Doug knew he was still here for a reason. The more we talked the more I could hear in his voice how his faith was strengthened through this experience. He shared with me stories about his faith, specifically encounters he had with a loving God.

Remember, Doug was an excellent athlete in high school. He was an intelligent, fun loving, easy to talk to, all-around good guy. That was his past. Fast-forward to today and Doug is still many of those things. He is also a husband, a father of two, a support system for his wife who is self-employed, and one of the world's best engineers. Chances are you have used something in your everyday life that Doug has worked on in some capacity.

If you ask Doug personally he would tell you he had it made. But he knew that something was missing. The more we talked it was obvious what was missing, which was God at the forefront of his life. He literally had a God-shaped hole in his heart.

After the heart attacks Doug made wholesale changes. He changed his diet drastically. He started working out. He looked at his relationship as a husband and father differently. Do not get me wrong; he loved his wife and children wholeheartedly, but he realized

*Just JESUS Them*

afterward what a gift and blessing they are. Doug did not want to take a chance that he would miss out on any of that later.

At the end of the day, the most important things to Doug are not all of the material possessions that he has been blessed with on this planet. It is not all the accolades he has received. It is his wife, his sons, his dogs, his friends, and also his faith that mean the most to him and his everyday walk.

Yes, Doug had a couple of heart attacks one day. He could have lost his life. But he did not. Instead, he has chosen to live his life every day since that near fatal one, with a heart that many wish they had, that no longer has a God-shaped hole in it.

***JESUSing moment>>> The saying 'you can't stick a square peg in a round hole' will help you understand the 'God-shaped' hole that we all have. We try to put things in that hole and nothing fills it. It may be for a time or a season, but there is always that yearning. That is because the only thing that can fit in that God-shaped hole is God. Wherever you find that longing and yearning, that is where God is missing. Would you choose today to fill it with God by showing His love to someone else?***

www.PocketFullOfFaith.com

## Day 96
*Weathering the storm.*

---

Your JESUSing Moment             Date

**Matthew 8:23–25 (NIV) Then he got into the boat and his disciples followed him. Suddenly a furious storm came up on the lake, so that the waves swept over the boat. But Jesus was sleeping. The disciples went and woke him, saying, "Lord, save us! We're going to drown!"**

Hurricane Katrina was one of the worst hurricanes to ever hit the United States in terms of loss. New Orleans was the focus of many people, especially the media, during and shortly after the hurricane. This was due to the engineering defects in walls that caused unexpected flooding of large areas of the city. These areas were under sea level, causing evacuations and the displacement of many people living there.

Ten months after the hurricane, I was leading a mission team to this still ravaged area. The focus for our trip was Waveland, Mississippi, a small town in the southern part of the state. This town is where the eye of the hurricane hit. The magnitude of loss there was beyond comprehension.

Every day of the trip brought more challenges and more destruction. As an example, boats rose more than 30 feet due to the water that came inland, only to settle back to the ground in the middle of heavily treed areas where they still rest to this day. They will forever stay as reminders of this tragedy, as there is virtually no way to get the boats from their resting place unless hundreds of trees are chopped down first.

Beyond the destruction were the people left behind who survived the tragedy. We had the opportunity to meet many of them. Few had any belongings. Most had lost family and friends, either to death or relocation.

Through it all we were overwhelmed by the message we received from those that remained. Many spoke of how their faith had been restored through the storm and strengthened after it. Others shared that in the most difficult hours, when power was lost, and the water had reached its high point, that the only choice they had was to turn to God.

One gentleman showed me the attic that he and his family ended up in after their first and second floor had filled with water. You could see the line of debris that was left from the water reaching its maximum height. It was at this time that the family cried out and God showed up for them and many others. The water started to subside. Eventually it left the attic. Hours later it had left the house completely. The gentleman realized that when all they had was God, when all they could turn to was God, that God was enough.

Somehow, through the worst storm they had ever seen, God had shown He was in control. At just the right time, this family, and many others, had weathered the biggest storm of their lives.

***JESUSing moment>>> Storms shape us. Who do you know that is in the midst of a storm right now? They need to know someone is out there and that they care. Be the calm in the storm that they need right now and JESUS them!***

*www.PocketFullOfFaith.com*

*Just JESUS Them*

## Day 97
*Seeing God.*

---

| Your JESUSing Moment | Date |
|---|---|

**Romans 1:20 (NLT) *For ever since the world was created, people have seen the earth and sky. Through everything God made, they can clearly see his invisible qualities—his eternal power and divine nature. So they have no excuse for not knowing God.***

Another mission trip I had the honor to lead was to an Indian reservation in Arizona. At the end of our trip, we took the team to the Grand Canyon as a thank you for all of their hard work. They had been a blessing while serving others, and this gave them a place and a time where they could reflect on the trip.

There is a particular place in the Grand Canyon where a rock sits on top of another rock, much like a golf ball sits on a golf tee. The two are not the same rock. They are separate, yet connected, and distant from the sides of the canyon. You cannot help but stop, look, and think: "How could that possibly happen?"

One of my students stood there for what seemed an eternity staring at the golf ball rock sitting on the tee rock. I came up next to him and asked him how he was doing. "How does that happen," he asked, pointing toward a rock. "What do you mean?" I asked him back. (All I saw was a bunch of rocks—it is the Grand Canyon, after all, and that is pretty much what you see. It is amazing, though, and a must-see live.)

"How does one rock stay on top of another rock for all this time and never moves? How did it get there? Who put it there?" he asked. These were all fair questions. He continued. "It is perfectly placed."

That night this student shared this story and when he finished, he ended with these words: "When I saw that, I knew God was real. Nothing else could have done that. Nothing."

The Grand Canyon is a place you have to see first hand to take in, well, everything. Pictures cannot do it justice, and they cannot make you stop and think. You need to be there to truly understand and know what I mean.

An amazing thing took place that day though. For the rest of the trip, this student started *LOOKING* for God. He told me had never done that before. He took so much of where he lived for granted. I asked him what he saw. A sunrise, a sunset, a full moon, a tree giving shade to a tired migrant worker, a river running through a canyon . . . he saw everything differently all because of two rocks. He saw everything differently because God had placed *one thing* at *one time* in history to meet *someone* at *another time* in history. When the two collided: BAM, he could not help but see anything *but* God.

**JESUSing moment>>> Many times we do not see God because we do not look at the beauty of his creation. We take it for granted. If we want to see God more, we need to start looking for Him more. Just so you know, he was never lost to begin with—we just got too busy to see the beauty he has surrounded us with in our every day lives, including the people in our lives.**

www.PocketFullOfFaith.com

## Day 98

Joshua 1:8 (NLV) says: "This book of the Law must not leave your mouth. Think about it day and night, so you may be careful to do all that is written in it. Then all will go well with you. You will receive many good things." What can you write about from this week that you did with God at your side? What blessings did you receive from those JESUSing moments?

*Just JESUS Them*

*www.PocketFullOfFaith.com*

*Just JESUS Them*

# Day 99
*Wanting less.*

---

Your JESUSing Moment                                                   *Date*

**Proverbs 30:8b (NLV) *Do not let me be poor or rich. Feed me with the food that I need.***

The son of a family friend turned nine years old recently. I wrote this on his birthday to serve as a reminder of how simple life can be. It is also a reminder of how easily 'things' can get in the way in our complex lives.

I was doing my own personal "dad survey" as I sat three of my kids down to share that Jacob had turned nine. I asked them this question: "What do you think Jacob asked for this year for his birthday?" Immediately, my soon to be 14-year-old said "A phone." My 16-year-old son, Jacob, replied "An iPad." My 11-year-old daughter's answer was "A Kindle Fire."

I found it fascinating that the first thought each of my kids had was a handheld device. We have all heard about the information age and how technology has controlled each of us. I wrote that sentence on my Mac Book Pro, with my cell phone sitting on the crook of my shoulder and my iPad next to me as it updated an application. True story.

It is a sad story, too.

We live in the richest country in the world. We have more freedom than we even realize. We can worship God or worship the world on a whim. We can get anything—all kinds of 'stuff'—whenever we wish. At the end of the day, it is just as described. It is just 'stuff.'

The older we get, the more we realize this fact. Knowing this, though, what do you think Jacob asked for his birthday? Stop for a second and ask yourself, what do you want for your birthday? If you were nine again, what would you want for your birthday?

What did he ask for on his last year of single digits? To have a fire in his back yard, to roast hot dogs over it, and for his family and friends to eat these his birthday meal. The "stuff" he wanted was simple, and he did not want it all to himself. He wanted his family and friends to share this with him on his special day.

What do you need to put down so you can be fed and feed others today?

***JESUSing moment>>> Every day is special to Jesus. It should be special to us, too. What simple act can you do for someone to show you care? Just JESUS them!***

www.PocketFullOfFaith.com

*Just JESUS Them*

# Day 100
*Being a light.*

---

Your JESUSing Moment                                    Date

**Luke 1:38 (ESV) Behold, I am the servant of the Lord; let it be to me according to your word.**

We all have someone in our life that has a special way about him or her. It does not matter what they say or do, they have a way of making you feel better about yourself or a situation you are going through.

Have you ever had someone you have never *actually met* who has that same effect on you? For me, that is Terri. Yes, I know her name. No, we have never met (that was at the time I wrote this—we have officially met since). If they put her in a line up and you and I had to pick her out of that lineup the first time, we would both have the same chance of getting it correct the first try. Yet, every time I have any communication with Terri, I walk away feeling better about whatever it is that is going on in my day.

How does someone impact people so positively? How does someone exude those kinds of emotions without ever actually seeing or touching the person on the other end?

It starts with a choice. At some point in her life, Terri made the decision that she was going to be kind every time she made contact with another person, even if it was not physically. She made the choice to be enthusiastic, energetic, and helpful in all of her ways. For me, personally, since we only speak through e-mail, this also means the way she writes to me. Terri is the master of the exclamation point and of interjecting some fun into her email messages (she may not even realize she is doing it, although I believe she is).

At the end of the day, she can shut down her computer knowing she controlled what she can control. She chose her words. She chose to be kind. She chose to do as Jesus did and treat every person as she would like to be treated. She chose to be a servant. She chose to live by God's Word.

It is not an intermittent choice, either. For Terri, it is intentional. It is a lifestyle. It is what we have called throughout this book 'JESUSing others.'

It seems simple enough. Will you and I choose to follow Jesus' lead, as Terri did and does every day? This is such a simple way to Jesus others. But it starts with Terri, or you, or me, making the decision to do so.

It is a personal choice that each individual makes. Part of that choice is being a light to others you may not even know, and may never get the opportunity to meet.

*JESUSing moment>>> Would you make the choice today to Jesus others through areas someone would least expect? It could be via e-mail, a text message, or some other type of social networking. Choose to treat others with the same words that you hope to receive—even to those you may never have the opportunity to meet face to face!*

www.PocketFullOfFaith.com

*Just JESUS Them*

## Day 101 (Part 1)
*Breaking the ice.*

---

Your JESUSing Moment                                    Date

**1 Corinthians 9:3 (NIV) *This is my defense to those who sit in judgment on me.***

I had a very odd day recently. Everyone I saw made eye contact with me and smiled. It was so refreshing that people took the time to notice me. Not only did they notice me, some actually acknowledged me. Others even spoke to me and we had very nice conversations.

That started my mind turning. Why are there days where people can be so nice and other days seem not to care at all? It just happened that this was on a Tuesday. Maybe it was because the Monday blues were gone. Maybe Tuesday is a day where people are the happiest. Maybe the sun was shining. I could not come up with an answer.

As I pondered this in my mind, I held the door open for two separate women. One was a little older and one was younger. The one who was younger smiled and looked away quickly. The older woman smiled at me and stared a little longer. Neither said a word, yet, through their actions, both of them were telling me something was not quite right.

As I was heading out of the building I started to take a closer inventory of myself. I looked at my shoes and the clothes I was wearing to make sure that everything matched.

It did.

However, there was one problem. The shirt I had on that day I was wearing inside out. It was then that I realized the people who had been so nice to me that day were actually feeling sorry for me.

*Just JESUS Them*

I could not help but laugh at myself. The funny thing to me was the reason my shirt was on inside out. I will share that tomorrow, but first; let's do something together.

I want you to prepare to JESUS someone. After you read today's DO-votional, hopefully a place or a person came to your heart and mind. Now I want you to get ready physically to go. Before you leave, I want you to walk to a mirror. Take a look at yourself. Do NOT be critical. You are NOT too short or tall, you are NOT too young or old, and you are NOT too big or small. What you see looking back at you is the person God has made and that God loves. When you realize this vital point, you are ready to go and Jesus someone.

Lastly, before you leave, take one last look. Do this for me. Check and make sure your shirt is not on inside out. If it is, trust me, people will notice.

***JESUSing moment>>> I just gave you the JESUSing moment you can use. All you have to do is follow the steps and make sure your shirt is on the right way!***

www.PocketFullOfFaith.com

*Just JESUS Them*

# Day 102 (Part 2)
*Breaking the ice.*

Your JESUSing Moment                                      Date

**Matthew 4:19a (The Voice) "Jesus: Come, follow Me."**

Yesterday I shared with you that I am not the world's most accurate dresser. If, for some reason, today you are starting this devotional for the first time, make sure you go back and read yesterday or you will be confused as to why we started the story in the middle. When we ended yesterday, I shared that my shirt was on inside out. There was a reason for this. I am not saying it was a good reason, but there was a reason.

I had taken a shower the night before and after taking a shower, I put on this dreaded shirt. My wife was sleeping and I did not want to wake her. I opened the drawer and felt for a shirt and put it on over my head. I realized I had put it on backward because of how it felt on my neck. The logical step would be to pull your arms back into the shirt and turn it around and then make sure it felt right on around my neck after putting it on the rest of the way. Rather than just turning it around, though, I pulled it up over my head, turning it inside out and THEN I turned it around and put it back on the 'right way.' It also happened to be one of those shirts that had no tags in the back of it. I was tired and it was comfortable and felt right around my neck, so all I was thinking about was going to sleep.

The next day when I was rushing around, I realized I was behind and had an appointment in 10 minutes that was a 15-minute drive away. I ran upstairs to grab a pair of sweatpants that matched the shirt color I was wearing. I was heading to meet a friend of mine at a local gym. I still never thought to look at the shirt other than the color. I had already sealed my demise.

The more I thought about it the more I laughed. But then it dawned on me. People rarely look at one another to acknowledge their existence. Not one of the people I talked to that day let me know

*Just JESUS Them*

my shirt was on inside out. If I had noticed someone wearing his or her shirt inside out, I would let someone know. The reason for that is *I* would not want to walk around all day with my shirt inside out. I met no one like me that entire day.

This led my thoughts to how many people struggle with breaking the ice when it comes to talking about their faith. The inside out shirt trick (trying to start a craze here, so work with me) was a perfect way to get people to talk to me. It could be a goofy hat, mismatched shoes, crazy socks, or wearing your clothing inside out (too late for you, the patent is pending). People will notice, and give you the opportunity to share why you chose to wear what you wore on this day. It is an easy way to start a conversation that could lead to you JESUSing someone else, even if they think you are crazy or challenged in some other way.

It is now your turn. Get dressed and get ready. Time to go break the ice!

***JESUSing moment>>> Wear something that is a little bit different where people cannot help but ask you what or why you are wearing it. Then you can blame it on this devotional. It is a way for you to break the ice and reach out to others and show your faith. Have fun with it and get ready to share and live your faith!***

www.PocketFullOfFaith.com

*Just JESUS Them*

# Day 103
*Avoiding distractions.*

---

Your JESUSing Moment               Date

**Hebrews 12:12 (NLV) So lift up your hands that have been weak. Stand up on your weak legs.**

If you have ever seen the Disney/Pixar movie "Up" there is a scene in it where a dog is able to speak like a human being. He is so focused one second yet so distracted the next. He is having a conversation with two people he just met when suddenly something runs by that completely diverts his full attention. "Squirrel," the dog says, looking away quickly in the direction of the squirrel. He then turns back to the conversation with the humans, forgetting where they left off while they were talking.

Many of us are like this. We can be laser-focused one second, and completely on to something else the next. Many people claim this to be either ADD or ADHD. They have never been officially diagnosed with either disorder, but, it is easier to claim one of these than to face the fact they are just easily distracted.

If you were to speak to these people one-on-one, you would find that these distractions drive them crazy. In our high technology, fast-paced world, this is commonplace. It could be a TV show, the Internet, smart phones, social networking, or literally a squirrel. Everywhere you go there are distractions.

For each of us these are weaknesses. They also become excuses.

They are excuses for not showing our faith.
They are excuses for not focusing on our faith.
They are excuses for not loving and showing Jesus to others.

Here is what I want to challenge you to do, and I want you to be focused on these, exclusively. First, put down the e-mail, smart phones, and turn everything off around you. This may include people in any type of distractions! It could also be music, television, video games, or any type of noise. Next, make a list of the

## Just JESUS Them

things that so easily distract you. Now ask yourself this question: am I allowing these distractions to keep me from caring for others? Here is the follow up to that question, if you are still with me. Am I so focused on the busyness surrounding me that I am losing focus on the people around me?

Whether we want to admit to it or not, these are weaknesses. The verse today reminds us to lift up your hands if you have been weak. It also tells us to stand up on our weak legs. If you and I are going to stand up on those weak legs, we may as well strengthen them by walking to someone and having a one-on-one conversation.

Avoid any distractions and take this as a sign to reach out to someone that you know is in need.

*JESUSing moment>>> We all have weaknesses. It is easy to become distracted in our fast-paced world. Why not put everything away and have that one-on-one conversation with someone today? It is something you are probably longing for, which means the person on the other end may be longing for it, as well!*

www.PocketFullOfFaith.com

*Just JESUS Them*

# Day 104
*Having a "Plan B".*

---

| Your JESUSing Moment | Date |
|---|---:|

**1 Samuel 20:17 (NIV) And Jonathan had David reaffirm his oath out of love for him, because he loved him as he loved himself.**

Jody and Jerry were true friends. Their friendship started and centered on a game they both loved: baseball. What really grew their friendship was what they built together, and a trait they both would forever share. Jody and Jerry always gave from their hearts.

For Jody, his story meant becoming one of the most successful business stories you might have never known. He literally became a "CROWN", the highest achievement possible, for Amway in the early 1980s. For Jerry, this meant building and naming an actual baseball diamond, CROWN field, after his friend, Jody. They both shared in the success they lived and gave to these diamonds.

The team they had built this field for together, in the town I currently live in, was known as the Manchester A's. When the team first started as a baseball travel team, they had no field to call home; that was when Jerry came up with 'Plan B'. Rather than rent or find an existing field, they would build and run their own. When Jerry brought Jody to the place where he wanted to put the field, all Jody saw was a swamp. Jerry, however, saw it differently; he saw what would be known to this day as CROWN Field. It was named, aptly, for his friend, Jody, and the success he had in the world of business through Amway. Jody saw the same in Jerry, as he named part of his business after his friend Jerry and his ways: "Plan B". No matter the intended direction of the day, Jerry always had a "Plan B". Make no mistake about it; many successful teams would play on this field for decades to come: but the reason it was built was because of two friends who had a common interest, had a passion, and believed they could make a difference. They gave of themselves, their resources, and their time: and a bond grew between the two that would last an eternity.

*Just JESUS Them*

Their story struck me as Jody shared the backstory on the field. My son was one that played on this field, as was Jerry's son, too, and so many others. For all of us, we smiled and relished in the words that Jody shared. The reason for him sharing this story with us was because Jody was speaking at Jerry's funeral, as he had lost his battle with cancer. Jody shared the value of a friend. He shared the dreams they had, the beliefs they upheld, and the diamonds they had both became. It was a bond many wish they had; yet few achieve in this lifetime.

At the end of the day, Jody lost one of his crown jewels; but, he also knew that heaven gained a new jewel to add to all of its beauty. Jerry gave of himself while here on Earth; part of that giving was to his friend Jody. Jody continues to give of himself and his resources. Knowing Jerry waits for him in heaven, Jody is at peace with this eventual, eternal "Plan B".

*JESUSing moment>>> There is a hope that we will all be in heaven one day; but, is this a hope we share with those closest to us? Do we walk and talk with them daily as if we are walking to heaven together? Or, do we sit back and hope that our friend knows, and that they have an eternal "Plan B".*

www.PocketFullOfFaith.com

## Day 105

Peter writes at the beginning of 2 Peter 3:16a (NIV): He writes the same way in all his letters, speaking in them of these matters. He goes on to state that there are difficult things to understand about what he writes. As you near the end of the book, I am sure there are times when it has been difficult to get through and work through. Remember, though, that when you Jesus others, they are moments that will always matter.

*Just JESUS Them*

www.PocketFullOfFaith.com

*Just JESUS Them*

# Day 106 (Part 1)
*Sharing Jesus not the church.*

---

Your JESUSing Moment                                      Date

**John 13:34b (NLV) *You are to love each other. You must love each other as I have loved you.***

People love Jesus. They hate the church.

Think about those two statements. Do you believe both of these to be true? Do you believe neither of these to be true? Or do you believe one, but not the other?

Study after study show that people believe both of these statements to be true. Sadly, thousands of years after Jesus came to this earth, loved people, and offered them a place in eternity by trusting and believing in Him, the church has lost its way. The public as a whole views the very institution that was built on God's son and His resurrection, i.e. the church, as one that has become more and more like the ones Jesus challenged to change their ways.

This group was led by the Pharisees, which, in the New Testament, would be considered the religious ones. They made the rules. They prayed loudly on the street corners. They looked down on people that did not follow the rules *they* established. The only real way was their way.

Yet Jesus challenged that way.

The amazing fact was the Pharisees all along were looking for the Messiah. Jesus did not fit the qualifications of what they were looking for and what they had been taught to seek. They wanted a warring king who would take the power away from the Roman Empire. They hoped he might ride in on an elephant with a large army behind him to save HIS chosen people, the Jews.

Instead, Jesus came in on a colt. He was loving, kind, gentle, and caring. He had no army. Jesus healed people any day of the week,

*Just JESUS Them*

including the Sabbath. He met people at the lowest times of his or her life. He humbled himself before the masses and to people personally. Jesus died a gruesome death on the cross. It was meant to mock Him and crush the spirit of His followers, with the intent that no one would ever hear His name again. The problem was, Jesus happened to show up three days later, alive. Remember, this was *after* he died. He showed up to one, two, then tens and even hundreds. Many were there when He died. No one could deny that He lived again. All of this happened because He loved people.

If you want to know how Jesus loved, read about the things He did in the Gospels. Whether it is Matthew, Mark, Luke, or John, Jesus loved others. All He asked in return was for us to love these people in our lives just as He loved us.

What is not to love? (The church is an entirely different story-more on that tomorrow.) In the end, though, people cannot help themselves. They hate the church. But, they do love Jesus.

***JESUSing moment>>> It may seem like a difficult assignment to Jesus people every day. He made the choice to each person He came in contact with every day. It is the same choice you and I can make with every person we see and meet.***

*www.PocketFullOfFaith.com*

*Just JESUS Them*

# Day 107 (Part 2)
*Sharing Jesus not the church.*

---

Your JESUSing Moment          Date

**Acts 11:26b (NIV) The disciples were called Christians first at Antioch.**

People love Jesus. They do not love the church.

Study after study shows these statements to be true. The studies on the church have shown that we have somehow missed and forgotten the words and actions that Jesus shared with His disciples. Too many churches became more like the Pharisees and less and less like Jesus every day. It has gotten worse as the years have passed. Church attendance has dropped year after year, yet more and more people now consider themselves 'Christians.'

What I find funny are those who *never* called themselves Christians. Who would they be? The disciples. Jesus never called his movement anything special. It never had a name. Decades after his death and resurrection, before they were first called Christians, people were known by the way they lived. This movement was literally known as 'The Way.'

'The Way" used whatever resources they had to help others. They worked together and whatever they made went to feed and clothe others. They worshipped together in houses and public places, such as by the river, a town center, or a city gate. They were not ashamed. They were passionate. They loved. They were kind. They were everything Jesus was and is to us today.

What changed all of this you ask? The answer is simple. The church changed. God did not.

Rules were made and followed. Guidelines were established and never crossed. Commandments were added to the original, biblical commandments, and only enforced inside the church walls. By-laws were written, constitutions constitutionalized, and the church of the modern world was established.

*Just JESUS Them*

We have been missing the message of Jesus ever since.

If a church event or person in the church has scarred you, I feel for you and want to tell you those of us in the church today are sorry this happened. Realize this, though: not every church is like this today. There are those who understand it is about making disciples in Jesus' name. They understand it is in His name and not theirs. They also know what it means to love others as Jesus loved and loves us.

Maybe it is time to get back to being a part of the solution. This may be as part of the church or outside of its walls. Regardless, it all starts by JESUSing others, not CHURCHing them.

*JESUSing moment>>> How do you get out of a funk? Loving others. Regardless of past hurts, failures, or struggles, the best medicine we can all take daily is JESUS. Don't stop there. Make sure someone else gets that same medicine today through your loving, JESUSing words and actions!*

*www.PocketFullOfFaith.com*

*Just JESUS Them*

# Day 108
*Living for a cause.*

---

Your JESUSing Moment                                     Date

**Luke 12:25/Matthew 6:34 (NIV) "And can any of you by worrying add a single hour to your own span of life? ... So do not worry about tomorrow, for tomorrow will bring worries of its own. Today's trouble is enough for today."**

There is one thing I know for certain about you and me. We both live for a cause. Whether we realize it or not, have ever considered it, or even thought about it, there is something that drives us in our lives and gives us a reason to wake up every day and continue.

There is one cause that is near and dear to my heart. It is not a cause that I live for daily, but is a cause that I support. It started over a decade ago when a friend of mine lost a loved one. The loved one lost a battle with cancer. Instead of resting with the memories of this loved one, a cause was started. Through it, their memory lives through to this day.

*Showcase for the Cure* is put on each year at Walsh Jesuit High School in Stow, Ohio. Walsh Jesuit is a college preparatory school known for its academics and service. It is also known for this cause. Each year, the coach of the Walsh Jesuit baseball team, Chris Kaczmar, hosts it. Each year a different person or family is the honored guest. That family chooses where *all* the money raised goes to in the form of cancer research. The showcase centers on baseball, but its real beneficiary is the battle to cure this disease. College coaches and scouts come from all over the nation to watch these young prospects. For the prospects the camp is free. The only monies accepted are from donations.

Division I and Division II baseball coaches and their programs are well represented at this event. Speakers are chosen to help the young prospects in their growth as a baseball player as a potential, future college athlete. The best part of the day is when the honorary family is recognized. The outpouring of love, affection,

*Just JESUS Them*

and compassion is contagious. It brings some hope in the battle against a disease of which there seems no hope. A battle that, for many, goes on daily unrecognized. On this special day, however, on a high school baseball field in the corner of the school campus in Northeast Ohio it is recognized.

Hundreds and hundreds of people flock to the Showcase for the Cure every year. They flock to the field. They flock to the families that have been affected by this disease that knows no bounds. They come for the cause in hope of a cure.

This is a cause many live for every day. Sadly, it is also a cause that many have lost their lives in the process. Does that mean they will stop fighting and living for this cause? No.

In a school known for its faith and for preparing others to reach the world, this cause is one worth fighting for every day. It is one reason my friend Chris wakes up every day. It is part of a lifelong cause as he does his part in fighting this battle.

*JESUSing moment>>> We all live for a cause. It is part of what gets us out of bed every day. How can you use the cause you live for daily to love, care for, and reach others?*

*www.PocketFullOfFaith.com*

*Just JESUS Them*

# Day 109
*Gaining Trust.*

---

Your JESUSing Moment                                    Date

***John 14:1 (NLT) "Don't let your hearts be troubled. Trust in God, and trust also in me.***

You are about to learn today about the trust bank. This is something that was shared with me long ago. I tried it and it has held true over and over again. You can use this with your kids. You can use this with your spouse. You can use this with coworkers, fellow students, friends, or any relationship you have in your life!

I believe God uses it with us.

Here is how the trust bank works. Over time you naturally build trust. The longer you know a person and the more they prove trustworthy—meaning worthy of trust—the more they fill their 'trust account.' It is natural for us to trust them with more and more as this account grows.

The perfect example of this is the 16-year-old who just got his or her driver's license. At first they want to drive everywhere. As a parent, we do not allow this. They start by driving to the store on their own to get milk or bread for us. The next time they may be allowed to go to the gas station a mile further down the road. The next week they may drive to church. The next step is to have one person with them in the car, then two or three. Eventually, they may even drive to another city or county to go to a game or event. As they have succeeded in each of these, and do not get into any trouble or accidents, the trust grows. Because of the trust that is built, they are allowed to do more, with more people, until eventually driving is second nature.

Notice that building trust takes time. The deposits into the trust bank are done slowly and build slowly. However, should the same 16-year-old get a ticket or get into an accident, the withdrawal from this same account are immediate and in much larger amounts. It may be to the point they have to start completely over in building that trust again.

We did this for our children when they first started to walk. We did this for our children when they first learned how to ride a bike. We did this for our children when they started to go outside of the yard or to a friend's house. It is part of every facet in every relationship of our lives.

It is also that way with God. Like *every* relationship, it is a two-way street. We are called to trust. In turn, we build that same trust. How are you adding to your trust bank daily?

*JESUSing moment>>> Where is God trusting you today that you have not even considered? Time to build some trust and add to the trust bank as you go and Jesus that someone!*

www.PocketFullOfFaith.com

*Just JESUS Them*

# Day 110
*Taking accountability.*

---

Your JESUSing Moment　　　　　　　　　　　　　　　　Date

***Ecclesiastes 4:9 (NLT) Two people are better off than one, for they can help each other succeed.***

I used to work for a global company in Northeast Ohio. They were very big on training their employees in many different situations. I remember being asked this question in one of those trainings. It has stuck with me to this day: is it better to take accountability or to hold someone accountable?

Before you answer this question, think about the difference in the two terms. Taking accountability means you are taking ownership. Holding someone accountable is focusing on the other person and not yourself. Too often in our society we worry and focus on others. I am not sure why that is since the only ones we can really control are ourselves.

God has made it abundantly clear in his Word the importance of discipleship. Often times when you read about the disciples in the Bible you find them together. They are side-by-side listening, learning, and loving others together. When each of the disciples were finally ready to go on their own, Jesus sent them out two-by-two.

Why did Jesus do this? What is the value in it?

There re many reasons why. It gives us confidence. There is strength in numbers. It gives us a person to turn to in the good times and bad. Mostly, it takes us from holding others accountable to taking accountability.

As you are reading through this book day-by-day, hopefully you are finding daily challenges to make a part of your day. What if you had someone that was alongside of you doing the same thing? Would it not be exciting to be able to call that person each day when you took the time to Jesus someone? Would it not also be

*Just JESUS Them*

a challenge if they called you to share their moment when they JESUSed someone that day, especially on those days where you do not feel like taking the steps to do so?

Taking accountability means you focus on yourself and your walk. Having someone alongside of you, a.k.a. a fellow disciple, gives you someone to hold you accountable. If I asked you the question would you rather take accountability or hold someone accountable, what would your answer be?

When it comes to making the time to Jesus others, the answer is a simple, yet personal one: I need to do both. I need to take accountability. I also need someone in my life who will hold me accountable.

*JESUSing moment>>> You may have heard the term "accountability partner." I share that term because I have one in my life. His name is Ben. I wrote this devotional on his birthday. It is a reminder to me to take accountability every day and Jesus someone. It is also a reminder that I have him in my life to hold me accountable, as well.*

*www.PocketFullOfFaith.com*

*Just JESUS Them*

# Day 111
*Knowing whom we serve.*

---

**Your JESUSing Moment**      Date

***Joshua 24:15b (NLT) But as for me and my family, we will serve the Lord.***

One of the most frustrating conversations I have centers around the church. To be even more specific it centers on denominations. Baptist, Presbyterian, Catholic, Methodist, Christian, you name it I have had the conversation about what they "believe."

There are so many people who have been burned by the church or denominations over time. This pushes people away, but eventually they come back and want to talk. I know when it is coming. The conversation starts off with something like this: "What does your church believe about . . ."

My hat is off to so many people that have been devoted to their church for so long. Too often, however, the devotion is to the church and not to Jesus. When I sit down with people and I ask them what the Bible says about denominations, they rarely have as answer. Many do not realize that denominations are not in the Bible. The word Catholic is in the Bible, but is lower case. It means universal. The word Christian is in the Bible, but it was originally meant as a derogatory term. The word Baptist is in the Bible because of John the baptizer. None of these were churches or denominations in the Bible. So, if you ask what the belief system of a disciple of Christ should be, regardless of his or her professed denomination, then you have to turn to the words Jesus.

Here is what every denomination and every church needs to focus on, according to the New Testament: loving others and making disciples. Both of these come with disclaimers, however, and these tend to be forgotten quickly. We are called to 'love others' with the intent of doing this the same way Jesus loved others. We are called to 'make disciples' in the name of the Father, Son, and Holy Spirit. Too often we get into pastor worship, song leader worship, elder

*Just JESUS Them*

worship, self worship, church worship, and, of course, denominational worship. In other words, we end up replacing the most important piece of the entire puzzle when it comes to our relationship with God: His son Jesus.

If you are someone who has been burned by the church, I am sincerely sorry that this happened. Remember, though, at the end of the day, it is not the church that we should be serving. It is others. Do not get me wrong; there are many wonderful churches. I love the local church. I pastor one. When we alienate others because of rules, traditions, and denominations, we miss the message of who Jesus is and whom we serve.

Remind yourself every day of whom it is you serve. Do as Jesus did. Love as Jesus loved. Make disciples in his name. Not yours. Not the churches.' To keep your self on that track, start with this reminder every day: "as for me, personally, I will serve the Lord."

*JESUSing moment>>> Who or what is it you will serve today? JESUSing others is as simple as serving the Lord. YOUR choice! YOUR Lord!*

*www.PocketFullOfFaith.com*

## Day 112

Chronicles 28:19 (NIV) it states: "All this," David said, "I have in writing as a result of the Lord's hand on me, and he enabled me to understand all the details of the plan." The more we love others, the more we write these moments down when we met that person and God each day, the more we start to understand the plan God has for each of us individually.

www.PocketFullOfFaith.com

*Just JESUS Them*

## Day 113
*Spending your resources.*

---
Your JESUSing Moment                                     Date

**1 John 2:7 (NLT) Dear friends, I am not writing a new commandment for you; rather it is an old one you have had from the very beginning. This old commandment—to love one another—is the same message you heard before.**

If I gave you a $86,400 right now what would you do with it? Wait it gets better. What if I said you had the whole day to spend it and then tomorrow I was going to give you another $86,400 to spend? Wait, it gets even better. What if every day of this week, month, and year I would give you $86,400 to spend anywhere you wanted? Yes, it gets better still. What if I made you that promise that I would give you $86,400 to spend every day for the rest of your life?

What would you do with it?

Before you move forward reading the rest of the devotional I want you to stop and ponder what you would do with all that money every single day. Now here is the catch. You have to spend all of the money each day before you can move on to the next day. And, you do not get to keep any of the extra. Whatever you have at the end of the day is wasted and gone forever.

That would be challenging for each one of us. Sooner or later we would take the money for granted. Eventually we would have all that we needed and we would start to give it away to others. We would give it to those who need fed. We would give it to charities. We would send it to faraway places or people who are starving or where natural disasters have taken place. Occasionally we would have needs and we would fill them. But we would also realize we have this wonderful opportunity to help others with these resources. At some point for each one of us enough is enough and we would have to give it away.

*Just JESUS Them*

Now, let's change the equation. What if I said you were already receiving this every day and you did not realize it? Instead of dollars that I am giving you, God is giving you time. What would you do with it?

You would fill your day with things you think you need. You would work or go to school. You would go shopping. You may exercise. You would go to a movie or start a hobby. Sooner or later you would realize that you are only investing into yourself. If somebody asked you for 2,400 seconds of the 86,400 seconds you have would you give it to him or her?

What if God asked you for those 2,400 seconds? Would you set it aside for him? The most important resource that God has given each and every one of us we all have the exact same amount. What we do with it is our choice. Where we spend it is up to us. Remember, though, that God commanded each of us to pour it into others.

Would you go and spend 2,400 seconds to Jesus someone?

***JESUSing moment>>> Make the most of the most precious resource we all have the exact same amount of every day: time. Jesus someone who has this same resource!***

www.PocketFullOfFaith.com

*Just JESUS Them*

# Day 114
*Making a choice.*

---

Your JESUSing Moment Date

**John 21:17-18 (NLT) A third time he asked him, "Simon son of John, do you love me?" Peter was hurt that Jesus asked the question a third time. He said, "Lord, you know everything. You know that I love you." Jesus said, "Then feed my sheep."**

A man had a dream once that he was walking down a hallway. At the end of the hallway were two doors. A voice from above told him to look inside one of the two doors. He chose the door on the left and opened it and looked inside. In the center of the room was a table. At the table sat two people. They were malnourished to the point you could only see their bones. In front of each of them sat a large pot full of food. The problem was they could only eat it with a spoon. The spoon was tied to each person's arm. It was so long that they could bring the food to the top of the pot. Each person could not bend their arm enough to get the food into their mouth. Because of this they continued to starve. They sat there and grumbled and complained the entire time.

This was very unsettling to the man. After watching this for just a few minutes he stepped out of the door and closed it. He paused for a few moments thinking about what he just witnessed behind the door. At that moment he heard the voice again.

"Now look behind the other door," the voice said.

The man was very hesitant at first. The vision of what he had just seen was still in his mind. He slowly turned the doorknob and opened the door on the right. In the center of the room set a table. The same pots with the same food were on the tables. The same spoons were tied it to the arms of the people sitting at the table. Yet there they were laughing and enjoying their time together and all of them were eating heartily. There was no complaining, no grumbling, and no moaning. Everyone ate to his or her heart's content. The food never ran out.

## Just JESUS Them

The reason for this was simple. Instead of trying to feed his or her own mouth, the people made a choice. They chose to feed one another. One person would take the food out of their pot and reach the spoon across the table to feed the person across from them. The person across the table, in turn, would do the same for the person that just fed them. They chose to help one another. Because of this, everyone was well fed, content, and willing to share. Being well fed, they could not help but talk and enjoy their time with one another.

The man shut the door. The voice spoke to him and asking this question: "If you had to choose to spend your time in your life behind one of these two doors which would you choose?" The man did not have to think for more than a second. He would choose the door to the right where the people worked together.

The voice spoke again and said: "This is the choice you make every day of your life with all the people that you come in contact with: family, friends, and strangers. The door you choose to open is the door you choose every day of your life."

***JESUSing moment>>> Jesus shared in today's verses to love and feed His sheep. Which door will you choose today?***

www.PocketFullOfFaith.com

*Just JESUS Them*

# Day 115
*Praying with purpose.*

---

Your JESUSing Moment                                                Date

**1 Thessalonians 5:17(NLV) Never stop praying.**

How many times have you prayed for something and did not get the answer you wanted? Many times, this causes you and I to give up and stop praying, not only for the situation, but praying for anything. When asked why this is the case, the answers vary:

- God doesn't really care.
- God is not listening.
- God doesn't want me to have what I want.
- God is not paying attention.

Notice that all of these point to the same thing: God. They also point to the same conclusion. God is not overly concerned about us, personally. When I press people about these comments, the answer usually changes. They do not really want to blame God. They just do not feel he is all that interested in our every day lives. The answers change at that point:

- I get tired of praying for the same thing over and over and hearing nothing.
- I did not think it mattered because it was the same stuff on a different day.
- I stopped trying.
- I had nothing left in me to pray any longer.

A big reason for this book is for people like you and me. We pray and pray, we do the right things, we do what we feel God wants us to do, and then we are left with what seems to be a whole lot of nothing. This is why it is so important to reach and care for others. It is also why it is so important to never give up when we pray.

I once read about a man who was asked if he ever gained anything from all the time he prayed. His answer was a resounding, "NO!" He followed it with this comment: "In fact, I lost many things." The person asking the question stared at him, in shock. He smiled, and continued. "I lost being anxious, getting angry, being depressed, having insecurities, and fearing death."

The moral of his story is the driving force of the devotional for today. Praying is not about gaining but losing. In the end, what we lose ultimately ends up as gain.

Love others. But remember to never stop praying along the way.

*JESUSing moment>>> Do you have a prayer partner? Do you offer to pray for others? Do you ask others to pray for you? The JESUS them moment for today is to be able to answer yes to all three, and to never give up having a 'yes' as the answer to those all-important questions.*

www.PocketFullOfFaith.com

*Just JESUS Them*

# Day 116
*Including everyone.*

---

Your JESUSing Moment                                      Date

**2 Corinthians 9:8 (NIV) And God is able to bless you abundantly, so that in all things at all times, having all that you need, you will abound in every good work.**

Zach was different. When I say different, I do not mean in a bad way, either. Zach was fun loving, kind, loud, energetic, and an all-around nice kid. Sadly, he would not be the first kid you would choose on your baseball team, football team, or any athletic team. Zach has a handicap that keeps him from 'performing' at the same level as other 'normal' kids.

We were in our side yard on a cold day with teams even when Zach showed up. He had a glove, a ball, and a bat, and he was ready to play. Most of the kids in the neighborhood were older than Zach and this was a competitive game. I watched intently from a distance, as I wanted to see how the other boys would react. Zach came up and asked if he could play. One boy yelled out, "Which team wants Zach?" The two captains looked at each other as the teams were even. They quickly came to a decision. Zach would be an all-time hitter, as long as he was ok with that. Zach smiled and quickly agreed.

Zach struggled mightily in the game. Three strikes came quickly. On most days with this competitive crew, that meant outs came just as quickly. Not on this day. "Keep at Zach!" "You can do it!" "Watch the ball all the way off the bat!" "Throw your hands at the ball!" The boys from both teams were encouraging him with every swing. Strike four, five, and six came often, but an out was never counted. Zach would hit the ball eventually, and would run the bases the same way he did everything, with a smile on his face and with the energy of a two-year-old after a long nap.

The game went on with Zack running the bases and scoring at will. Sometimes guys got out behind him and he would be stranded on

## Just JESUS Them

a base. This did not matter to Zach as he ran back to the bats to get ready to hit again. Other times he scored and would take his place back in the hitter's line, cheering his teammates who were hitting or on the base paths.

I could not tell you who won that day. I am sure the captains that day could, although they would tell you different stories. What I can tell you is this: everyone enjoyed the game that day. Both teams played with laughter and competitiveness, and both teams loved playing with Zach on their side.

It takes the heart of a child to help us realize how much love God has for each of us. When Zach left, he thanked the boys. He grabbed his ball, glove, and his bat and walked toward his house with a couple other boys. Zach saw his mom and ran as hard and fast as he could to her. His mom hugged him with every part of her being, and listened intently as Zach gave her play-by-play on everything he could remember from the game.

***JESUSing moment>>> There is someone you know who feels left out. They sit at the outer edge of most moments, waiting to be included. Would you reach out to that person today and help them be a part of your world?***

www.PocketFullOfFaith.com

*Just JESUS Them*

## Day 117
*Overcoming addictions.*

---

Your JESUSing MomentDate

**1 John 4:19 (NLV) *We love Him because He loved us first.***

"Why are you here?" I asked.

"Because I am a heroin addict," Jacob answered bluntly.

"How old are you?" I asked next.

"Twenty-two," Jacob responded, "I will be twenty-three next week."

"How did you get here?" was my next question. We were having this conversation while sitting in a rehab/treatment facility.

"Bad decision after bad decision after bad decision," Jacob said, looking down at the table and fidgeting with nothing in particular. "I tried drugs when I was young. By high school I was getting in trouble all the time. By the time I was 16 I quit school altogether. Nobody seemed to mind." Jacob looked up at me with tears in his eyes. "I can't do it anymore. I can't keep living my way because I keep screwing it up."

"Why would you change now?" I probed.

"Because I know that my sister loves me. I know someone loves me. She hasn't given up on me. I no longer want to give up, either." Jacob confessed.

"You have been through this before, though. Why should she believe this time would be any different?" I asked?

"Because I am not going to do it my way anymore. I am going to do things God's way," was Jacob's reply.

30 minutes later, Jacob prayed and was finally resolved. Resolved with God. Resolved to change, according to what God teaches. Resolved not only as to who he was, but whose he was in God's

eyes. All because he had someone in his life that loved him, told him she would never give up on him, and, most importantly, that she believed God could and would help him do the same.

Jacob saw the reflection of God in his sister. His sister loved him because she knew Jesus loved her, and Jacob, first.

*JESUSing moment>>> People are lonely, discouraged, and feeling abandoned. Who can you reach out to that needs to know they are loved. You are reflecting Jesus when you take that step. Share with them that they are loved and you know that because you are loved first. That is what Jesus did for us all. Sadly, not many know this today. That is why it is up to us to share this amazing truth with someone today!*

www.PocketFullOfFaith.com

*Just JESUS Them*

# Day 118
*Battling depression.*

---

Your JESUSing Moment                                                         Date

**Hebrews 13:15 (NLV) Let us give thanks all the time to God through Jesus Christ. Our gift to Him is to give thanks. Our lips should always give thanks to His name.**

Depression is a widespread condition, affecting millions of people. It is NOT a sin, nor does it discriminate, meaning it affects both Christians and non-Christians. Those suffering from depression can experience a wide range of emotions. They can start with feelings of anger, leading to sadness and hopelessness. This can wear a person out physically, leading to fatigue and endless hours of sleep. A person dealing with depression can start to feel useless and even suicidal, losing interest in both people and events they once enjoyed. Depression is often triggered by life circumstances, such as being overlooked for a position, the loss of a job, family move, the death of a loved one, a divorce, or psychological problems such as mental or physical abuse.

There is another side to depression, as well. Clinical depression is a physical condition that must be diagnosed by a licensed physician. It may not be caused by unexpected life circumstances. It is also something that a person cannot just will away. Sadly, many people in the Christian community believe it is caused by sin. This is actually one of the oldest feelings in the Bible. Depression can sometimes be caused by a physical disorder that can only be treated with medication, spiritual guidance, and/or counseling. As a reminder, God can cure any affliction, disease or disorder. As an additional reminder, seeing a doctor for depression can be no different than seeing a doctor for sickness or an injury.

What does God say on the subject? Is depression in the Bible? Some feel that since it is not specifically stated, that it is a "gray area." Let us try a different approach. The verse for today reminds us to continually offer our praise to God. The Bible also tells us to be filled with joy. This means that God wants us to live a joyful life

*Just JESUS Them*

and it comes through our praise to God. If you are a person who deals with depression, this sounds good, but does not necessarily lead you to God, and to that joy.

What you have to understand is that over time, God CAN overcome ANYTHING, including depression. It can be remedied through prayer, Bible study, applying God's word to our daily lives, support or cell groups, fellowship with other believers, forgiveness, and Christian counseling. It starts by taking the focus off of our self. When we do this, our focus is inward, which takes us downward quickly. Instead, we need to turn our focus outward, which will take us upward to God just as quickly.

Today, like every day, let us take the focus off of us completely. Seek someone to spend the day with and care for, either one we know is depressed, or to help alleviate our own battle of depression.

*JESUSing moment>>> Some people you would least expect to be afflicted with depression are. We do not need to ask others it they struggle in this area. Rather, our goal should be to bring joy to others so they cannot help but see God in you.*

www.PocketFullOfFaith.com

# Day 119

Paul wrote in Galatians 1:20 (NIV): I assure you before God that what I am writing you is no lie. We all want to write in truth. Everything you have penned in this book on the days you wrote in your journal are the truths you shared when you not only loved others, you JESUSed them.

*Just JESUS Them*

www.PocketFullOfFaith.com

*Just JESUS Them*

# Day 120
*Investing in people.*

---

Your JESUSing Moment                                    Date

**Ecclesiastes 11:1–2 (The Message) Be generous: Invest in acts of charity. Charity yields high returns. Don't hoard your goods; spread them around. Be a blessing to others.**

"If you invest in people you will use things. If you invest in things will use people." I've heard the saying many times. It has made me stop and think about these words. I am not sure that I agree with that 100 percent.

I remember having this discussion with a friend of mine. They live in a beautiful house on a very scenic lot in a rural setting. There's nothing over-the-top about the house. It is very nice and you're very comfortable when you're there. They made the decision to add an in ground pool next to the house complete with a stamped concrete patio and a nice deck. It was an expensive addition all-around.

What is interesting is why they chose to have this addition. The easy answer is that they have two sons they were raising. That definitely weighed into the equation. But the main reason that they chose to do this was because of their youth group.

Rich and Karrie were youth workers at their church. The decision was there were going to build the pool but it was going to get used by more people than just the family. So we kept her week during the summer they open their house and their pool to the young people of the church. Many times this was during Bible studies and devotionals. Because of them using their gift of hospitality and using what God had blessed them with from the earnings, kids came to know Christ as your savior and chose to follow him in baptism.

We were talking about this one day when I asked Rich this question. Do you know every young person that came to know Christ

*Just JESUS Them*

through the use of your swimming pool? You never thought about that. But his answer was "No, there is no way of knowing." I smiled and said to him one day in heaven we will know. You may have people come up to you that you don't even remember that will thank you because you invested in them as a person. Yet through it all, it took the step of first investing in a thing to reach people.

So here is how I would change the quote from the beginning of the devotional. "It is okay to invest in things as long as you have people that you will love and reach in mind."

Simply put, Rich and Karrie, just like you and I, can invest in things if we are devoted to JESUSing others.

***JESUSing moment>>> what is it that you have you could use to Jesus others? It could be something big like a boat car or plane. It could be something small such as a video game. Whatever it is, what could you use today that would show someone else that you really love them?***

*www.PocketFullOfFaith.com*

*Just JESUS Them*

# Day 121

*Forgetting God.*

---

**Your JESUSing Moment**                                                  Date

**Mark 6:11 (NIV) *And if any place will not welcome you or listen to you, leave that place and shake the dust off your feet as a testimony against them."***

Many years ago my wife and I taught a class of ninth grade girls every Sunday morning. To tell you how long ago, let me say that at the time it was still called "Sunday School." One day, while teaching the lesson, someone sneezed. One of the girls immediately said, "Bless you." As we moved on with the lesson, another one of the girls said, "That's the problem with our world." We all stopped and looked at her. None of us was sure what was wrong with "blessing" another girl. She continued. "We take God out of everything. No one even takes the time to say 'God bless you.' He is the first thing we take out of everything. God is also the first one to take the blame. It is sad."

She was right.

Shortly after she made this statement, the Ten Commandments were removed from many schools. It was interesting that every time there was a school shooting, how many people blamed God. We took God out of the schools. Then we blamed him when a tragedy struck. We forced God out by law. Then we blamed God when he was not there to save everybody.

Fast forward over a decade later. I was taking my 14-year-old son to the doctor's office for a physical. As they gathered information on him, someone sneezed behind the receptionist. It was an open area so there were many workers there. Immediately, I said "God bless you." Most times when I do this, a person will smile and say "Thank you." The stare I received this time was anything but thankful. I smiled toward the lady who sneezed and was now staring at me. She turned away, saying nothing, and went back to her job. It was not as if I expected any thanks, but the acknowledgment she gave was very cold.

What should I do the next time a person sneezes? Should I do the simple thing? Should I just take God out of the equation? Should God take the blame for me if I choose to do so? My plan is simple. I will say "God bless you" the next time anyone sneezes. Remember that not everyone will agree nor accept God's message. Move on with your life with God. Move on and continue to do what at times may seem difficult. Remember that we were not called to be simple and to cast blame. We were called to love so people have the hope and opportunity to see a living and loving God.

May God bless you as you continue your journey.

*JESUSing moment>>> Where is it that you have simply taken God out of your every day life? Is it time to put him back in the small areas that do not seem like that big of a deal? If not, how long will it be before God starts taking the blame for the choices we have made to exclude God in our every day lives?*

www.PocketFullOfFaith.com

*Just JESUS Them*

# Day 122
*Playing to win.*

---

Your JESUSing Moment Date

**Ephesians 5:15 (NLV) So be careful how you live. Live as men who are wise and not foolish.**

A friend of mine has a saying: "If you are going to get kicked in the privates, it's ok, as long as in the end you win." If you are female, you have no idea what that means to a man. Some compare this pain to childbirth, although neither gender will ever truly know if that comparison is accurate. If you have experienced neither of these two, know this: it is going to hurt a lot. Period.

When it comes to our faith, many of us have every intention to play to win. We do the right things and attend church on Sunday and maybe even Wednesday or some other night. We might attend a small group or cell group in our community throughout the month. Some wake up early and read a devotional. Others start, end, or start and end the day with prayer. On the surface it seems as though we are not only playing the game, but, playing to win.

What are we actually doing to 'live our faith'? If you notice, all of the above examples are personal. They are all great examples of personal growth. They share how we have grown in our personal walk and are markers and evidence of that growth over time. They are all vital for us to be able to walk in our faith, be proud of our faith, and share with others in the safety of our faith-based groups.

That is when the hammer falls. Jesus never intended to walk in the safety of his faith. Jesus never lived the example of being safe in his walk. Jesus never loved others on a time schedule and behind closed doors, exclusively. If you look at what Jesus did and how he did it, you will find the exact opposite.

Jesus met the woman at the well in the hottest part of the day because she was humiliated and had to be there when no one else would. He spoke to a Samaritan knowing that the Jews were the chosen people, not the Samaritans. He turned over the tables in the temple, not just because of the money that the priests were making off of others, but because those same chosen people, the Jews, had taken away a place of prayer for the Gentiles. He did all of these things knowing that he would start his walk to the physical death that we all must endure. In other words, Jesus's walk led him to a pain beyond getting kicked in the privates or giving birth. Why would he do this for all of those people? Why did he choose to do this for you and for me? Why did he not just choose to play it safe, as most of us do every day?

Remember, in the end, Jesus won. He lives forever. Jesus gives each of us the opportunity to do the same. It is up to us as to how we play the game. Are we playing it safe, which is equal to getting kicked in the privates or the pain of having a child? Or, are we playing to win by caring for others when no one else will, even when it hurts, knowing that in eternity we experience no pain?

**JESUSing moment>>> Do not play it safe today. Reach someone where you least expected to and love them as Jesus would. (NOTE: do NOT put yourself or your life at risk doing so! Jesus lived dangerously but also did not put himself in the way of physical danger other than one time outside of the cross.)**

www.PocketFullOfFaith.com